AF380574

Repentance and the Mission of the Church

Repentance and the Mission of the Church

Making and Moving the People of God
into the Mission of God

W. RYAN VANDERLAND

WIPF & STOCK · Eugene, Oregon

REPENTANCE AND THE MISSION OF THE CHURCH
Making and Moving the People of God into the Mission of God

Wipf & Stock
An Imprint of Wipf and Stock Publishers
199 W. 8th Ave., Suite 3
Eugene, OR 97401

www.wipfandstock.com

PAPERBACK ISBN: 978-1-6667-6283-9
HARDCOVER ISBN: 978-1-6667-6284-6
EBOOK ISBN: 978-1-6667-6285-3

05/01/23

To my wife, Leslie, and our three boys, Levi, Jakob, and Jude,
and to all those who invested in me so I might make
a small contribution to the church

Contents

Introduction

As Christians, we know what we ought to be doing. We can quote the Great Commission found in Matthew 28:19–20. We might hear yearly sermons on Acts 1:8 and on how we ought to be witnesses for Jesus within our "Jerusalem" and to the ends of the earth. The question is not whether we know what we ought to do; the question is, "Why is it not working?" We know church attendance has been declining steadily over the last twenty years.[1] Not only is church attendance on the decline but the conversion of new believers has been falling year to year as well. In 2020, the Southern Baptist Convention, the largest Protestant denomination in the United States, reported that the number of baptisms reported was down almost by half from 2019 and had reached its lowest point since 1919.[2]

In response to these trends, one prominent Southern Baptist leader called for a renewed emphasis on "evangelism, missions, and church planting."[3] Other church leaders would seem likely to support these proposed solutions. Each of these certainly has a biblical grounding and a place within a strategy of taking the message of Jesus to a lost world. However, there is one biblical mandate missing. This could be the missing piece that makes the entire puzzle come together at last. This piece is repentance. And repentance is the focus of this study.

Why study repentance? Why, as a pastor, church leader, or church member, should you care about and study repentance? To anticipate the end at the beginning and to state the point of this work, repentance matters for many reasons, not least of which is because repentance leads us to mission. In much writing on repentance, what has been almost entirely missing is the connection between repentance and mission, both the mission of the

1. See Jones, "U.S. Church Membership," paragraph 2; and Pew Research Center, "Decline of Christianity."

2. Smietana. "Southern Baptist Decline," paragraphs 6–7.

3. Smietana, "Southern Baptist Decline," paragraph 8.

church and the mission of God, the *missio Dei*.[4] As we will see, the call to repentance stands as a central component of the mission of the church because it is central to the proclamation of Jesus as Jesus comes to embody the *missio Dei*. Thus, a rediscovery of repentance as a piece of the mission of the church can move the church to live out its God-given mission in a way that makes disciples and moves Christians within the church to live in God's mission.

Recovering a mission of repentance could be a discovery of a missional way forward as the church seeks to be witnesses and make disciples of Jesus. When we, as the church, know those around us are needy and broken because they have turned away from God, we are able to see them as Jesus saw them, as sheep, lost and in need of a shepherd. Then we are able to go, like God and with God, on mission to them. In other words, we turn to them as God turned to us. We become united in love with Christ and his mission. We feed the hungry, clothe the naked, visit the sick and the prisoners, love the unlovely, and in so doing we show the world what it means to turn to God and align ourselves and our lives with him (Matt 25:34–36).

Repentance, therefore, makes the people of God and moves them into the mission of God. Repentance sets the church and Christians apart in a culture where wrongs are excused and where repentance is lacking. This study makes this connection. It shows how refocusing the church on repentance, as a part of its mission because repentance is part of God's mission, can help the church to be both different and compelling and therefore missionally engaged with the culture, especially within the United States, during the twenty-first century. Additionally, as Jesus' gospel proclamation revolves around the kingdom of God, it has an eschatological emphasis as well. By "eschatological emphasis," I mean repentance not only calls individuals to turn away from sin, but also invites individuals and communities into the reality where Jesus reigns over the kingdom.

I hope this book benefits the reader in three specific ways. First, I want the reader to leave this book with a clearer understanding of the doctrine of repentance. Richard Owen Roberts begins his work *Repentance: The First Word of the Gospel* by saying, "The first word of the gospel is not 'love.' It is not even 'grace.' The first word of the gospel is 'repent.'"[5] Growing up in conservative evangelical churches, I of course heard the words "repent" and "repentance." Calls to repent were usually made within the context of

---

4. Our study will be bound to works on repentance written in English, with a primary focus on works on the doctrine and theme of repentance written over the last eighty years or so, beginning with William Douglas Chamberlain's 1943 work, *The Meaning of Repentance*.

5. Roberts, *Repentance*, 23.

personal salvation or within the context of repenting from specific sins. Beyond those two uses, repentance was rarely defined and never approached from the perspective that repentance could be a part of the very mission of God or of the church. Additionally, repentance, as I heard it taught within the church, was an action God demanded, otherwise I would be lost and dead in my sin. Such a belief was considered to be true even though the way and means by which I was to repent were not clearly articulated. Repentance was not taught as part of God's mission in the world. It was not something God actively participates in and is in the process of moving his creation toward. However, as I studied repentance and read the current scholarship, I kept seeing the connections between repentance and the mission of God and repentance and the mission of the church. As we proceed, we will see repentance is so much broader and so much more important within the life of the believer and the church than we have, perhaps, thought before.

Second, I want the reader to see the connection between repentance and discipleship. Repentance is not a doctrine merely existing in the realm of theory; rather it is a doctrine that becomes lived out in experience. As followers of Jesus, we can practice repentance and as we do we are brought closer to Christ and become more like Christ.

Third, my hope is for the reader to see how preaching and practicing repentance is vital for the church to be able to carry out its mission in the world. The message we proclaim as believers and as the church of Jesus Christ is that anyone and everyone has the opportunity to turn toward God because God has turned toward them. This message sets us apart from the culture but also makes the Christian message attractive to the culture. In a world of "cancel culture" and hollow apologies, the message of Jesus, preached by his church, is a message saying, "No matter who you are or what you have done, God turns to us so we can turn to him."

Unlike my childhood experiences in church, much of the current works and scholarship on repentance have focused on the definition of repentance, its role within certain biblical books or the Bible as a whole, or systematic theological approaches that have examined topics like "Seven Myths of Repentance" and "Seven Marks of Repentance."[6] We can gain insights from these works and will interact with them throughout the subsequent pages. Their foundations will be invaluable to our study while we also point out some of their weaknesses and make new connections between repentance and the mission of the church as it relates to the *missio Dei*, the mission of God.

---

6. See Watson, *Doctrine of Repentance*, and Roberts, *Repentance*.

To pursue this direction of study, we look at repentance in a broad interdisciplinary way. We want to see what repentance *meant* when the biblical writers used various Hebrew and Greek words to describe what we have termed in English "repentance." However, more importantly we want to see what repentance *means* for today and how a rediscovery of repentance influences the mission of the church. The desire of this work is to grasp repentance in a way that furthers our understanding of God and our relationship to him, as this is the basis of all theology. We use the Bible and reference the work of theologians, as well as make historical connections to rediscover why repentance matters within the church, within God's mission in the world, and how it points us toward God's ultimate ends.

There are two major strengths to this interdisciplinary approach. First, it allows us to interact with a wide variety of authors—not just theological scholars. Second, it allows us to see the connections between repentance and each of these disciplines to ultimately help us reach our goal of showing how repentance features as a central piece within the *missio Dei* and the mission of the church.

WHO IS THIS FOR?

The message of this book applies to the entire church; this includes pastors, as well as lay people. I believe mission applies to the whole church, not just to pastors, ministers, or church staff members. Since this work deals with the mission of the entire church in the world and how the church can recapture a lost piece of its mission, this work must be made available for the entire church community. That being said, the topic of this work may connect most readily to pastors who are interested in the broader mission of the church, as well as to church members who are invested in the mission and direction of the church. Therefore, my intention is to write in a way that makes the themes discussed accessible.

Those familiar with theological writing may find I am laying foundations that have already been laid; however, for some church members these foundations are necessary. These limited foundational discussions will also ensure we are building upon common understanding. Nevertheless, some assumptions must be made as an author about the reader. Throughout this work I assume the reader holds a basic understanding of the Bible. This includes an understanding of words like "Torah," what books are included in the "Prophets," and the definitions of words like "salvation" and "redemption" within a biblical context. Otherwise, much of the theological jargon that may be unknown to the general church member has been avoided. For those who desire additional content, the footnotes are key. Additionally, while we must discuss specific words found in biblical Hebrew and Greek, the reader will not be required to know the Hebrew or Greek alphabet, as these words are transliterated into English—as I have already done above.

As I must make some assumptions about the reader, some background knowledge of me, as the author, may also prove beneficial. I am approaching this work as an American, white, evangelical pastor. Thus, the kind of biblical interpretation herein, the kind of illustrations I use, and the theological assumptions I make reflect, to a greater or lesser degree, my own context and experience. I believe this work, including illustrations and applications, speaks across denominations, ethnicities, and religious experience. However, I must acknowledge, up front, the background from which these appear.

OUTLINE

Our study commences by examining repentance as mission in three parts. Part 1 explores the mission of God and the mission of Jesus. After an opening chapter where we survey the current scholarship on repentance with a view to understand where the conversation stands today and how we can move it into an unexplored area, we proceed in chapter 2 with God and God's mission in the world. This chapter shows one aspect of God's mission is turning or returning, both God's people turning/returning to him and God turning/returning to his people. Within this chapter, I look at sample passages throughout the Old Testament, beginning in Genesis, where I show that God's promise to Abraham, Isaac, and Jacob that they will return to the promised land links God's covenant of blessing the world with the calling of a people who turn toward him. Chapter 3 continues the discussion of mission by turning to the New Testament and the mission of Jesus. We examine Jesus' fourfold mission: seeking and saving the lost (Luke 19), calling sinners to repentance (Luke 5, 15), announcing the kingdom (Matt 4:17, Mark 1:15), and calling a people (Matt 11–12). All four are linked by either the direct call or within the context of repentance or turning.

Part 2 includes chapters 4 and 5. After showing both God's mission seen in the Old Testament and God's mission seen in Jesus within the New Testament involve a call to turn/return, I then show the biblical theme of repentance helps us define this mission. Within chapter 4, more voice is given to the scholars and theologians who have written on the topic to help us define what repentance means. Special attention is given to seeing repentance connected to turning from sin. After defining repentance, chapter 5 shows, from Acts to today, part of the mission of the church is to preach the message of repentance. We accomplish this by linking together the mission of the church and repentance through examining the role of repentance in Acts in the preaching of both Peter and Paul. Then we look at examples of the repentance/turning theme in the letters of Paul, specifically his calls to change lifestyle and behavior. Additionally, we note why a recapturing of repentance as part of the mission of the church is needed within the culture of American evangelicalism today.

Finally, in part 3 we draw the pieces together and seek to make application. Chapter 6 explores how embracing the mission of repentance leads the church into God's ultimate future. This future is defined by the kingdom of God, transformation, and a new reality. Within each of these eschatological realities, repentance plays an important role. The final chapter consists of a call to live as people of repentance within the church and rediscover the call to repentance as part of the mission of the church today. We discover how repentance begins with humility, is rooted in love, and turns one toward Christ. This chapter proposes that returning repentance as a central calling of the church today can help the church be disciple-making, loving, and forgiving. Thus, it is both a point connected with salvation and an ongoing process. We conclude by recognizing how repentance can also help the church stand apart from the current culture as we, as Christians, call men and women to participate in God's mission.

PART 1

1

Surveying the Landscape

As we embark on our journey, it is wise to review the current landscape of repentance as it has been explored in recent scholarship. Thus, I want to review three of the prominent ways repentance has been explored within recent discussions. Obviously, these are not the only three ways repentance has been explored in recent works—we reference more authors and works throughout our study—however, these give us a good introduction as we move forward. These studies were chosen because they constitute the newest, most scholarly, and most accessible works on repentance. Each was written in the twenty-first century, and two of the works are part of the New Studies in Biblical Theology series under general editor D. A. Carson. These three authors, and the works they represent, are illustrative of three ways of looking at the topic of repentance, and while they all contribute useful insights to the discussion, none of them individually or collectively connect repentance to mission in the way I am here. They do come close, however; thus this survey notes some preliminary contributions to our exploration, and emphasizes where our study builds upon their work, and addresses some of these studies.

UNDERSTANDING REPENTANCE BIBLICALLY: MARK J. BODA

Mark J. Boda, professor of Old Testament at McMaster Divinity College in Ontario, offers two works we must address because they comprise the fullest biblical theologies of repentance widely available today. There are relatively few contemporary works on repentance, and these two works place Boda as the foremost biblical scholar on the subject. Thus, Boda's work sets the table for much of our discussion. We'll look at Boda's contributions in chronological order. The first volume, *Repentance in Christian Theology*, is a collection of essays on repentance edited by Boda in conjunction with Gordon T. Smith.[1] The opening section of essays looks at repentance throughout the different divisions of the Bible: Torah, Prophets, Synoptic Gospels, and Epistles. These compositions review the use of repentance, either by noting uses of the words translated "repent" or "repentance" or by noting how the theme is used within these sections of Scripture. The works in this section are helpful and contribute to the biblical understanding of repentance presented in this study.

In one of the final essays in the book, Old Testament scholar Walter Brueggemann offers some conclusionary thoughts, including two that are vital as a launching point for this work. First, as Brueggemann reflects on the various definitions, connotations, and pictures of repentance seen throughout the preceding chapters, he concludes there arc both commonalities within the use of repentance throughout the Bible and Christian tradition as well as an "inescapable" and "imaginative diversity" found in the practice and understanding of repentance within the Christian faith.[2] As we see in more detail as we proceed, there is no singular definition for "repent" or "repentance," whether we are seeking a biblical or a theological definition. There are, however, similar themes seen throughout definitions and usages of the Hebrew and Greek words that create the doctrine of repentance. At the same time, the variety within the definitions of "repent"/"repentance" means we can explore repentance in a new light, while remaining true to the essence of the meaning found within the full scope of the biblical witness.

The second observation made by Brueggemann essentially begins by asking the question this work addresses, namely, what does the doctrine of repentance mean for the church and for the church's mission as a part of the mission of God? Within his comments, he says the question of how the church "[takes] up this great theme of penitence in a way that is pertinent to a culture that is a mix of conformity and autonomy" is the "next question" that must be answered.[3] Answering this question, he says, will add to the

---

1. Boda and Smith, *Repentance in Christian Theology*.

2. Brueggemann, "Summons," 349.

3. Brueggemann, "Summons," 349–50. Throughout Brueggemann's remarks, he uses "repentance" and "penitence" essentially as synonyms. The main difference between the two terms in Brueggemann is that penitence is the act of repenting.

"richness" of the study of repentance.[4] We want to make those connections and study its richness.

Mark J. Boda's second work of interest to this present study is *Return to Me: A Biblical Theology of Repentance*, authored solely by Boda and published in 2015. His purpose in the book is to "return to the Bible to offer a comprehensive overview of the theological witness of Scripture concerning the theme of repentance."[5] He accomplishes this goal admirably, especially when it comes to looking at repentance throughout the Old Testament. Boda's Old Testament survey is central to the discussion upcoming as we look at how we define repentance.

My critique of Boda's work on the theme of repentance comes when he turns his attention to the theme within the New Testament. There Boda spends only twenty-six pages on the entirety of the New Testament. Within Boda's section on repentance in the New Testament, he spends a few pages noting the theme through the Gospels, Acts, Epistles, and Revelation. Turning to theology, Boda briefly speaks to the connection between repentance and the kingdom of God preached by both John the Baptist and Jesus.[6] However, he does not examine this in detail. Additionally, while Boda does mention the church and the "Christian community,"[7] he does not present an ecclesiology of repentance or show its centrality to the message and mission of the church, either in the time of the New Testament or today. Within both of these works, Boda takes us on an important journey of understanding repentance; however, he merely glances off of important observations that are worthy of our exploration. As an Old Testament scholar, Boda spends a majority of his time in the Old Testament; however, this tells only part of the story. When Boda comes to the New Testament, he misses obvious connections between repentance and mission addressed in this work.

A LITERARY APPROACH: GUY D. NAVE JR.

Whereas Boda writes a fully biblical theology of repentance, Nave presents a "literary rather than a theological approach to understanding repentance in Luke-Acts."[8] The focus on Luke-Acts is because the two books contain twenty-five of the fifty-six occurrences of "repent" and "repentance" within the New Testament. In addition to examining the use of repentance within

4. Brueggemann, "Summons," 350.

5. Boda, *Return to Me*, 19.

6. Boda, *Return to Me*, 163–64, 181.

7. Boda, *Return to Me*, 185.

8. Nave, *Repentance in Luke–Acts*, 6.

the literary contexts of Luke-Acts, perhaps Nave's greatest contribution to the study of repentance comes from a secondary aspect of his work. Before looking at the New Testament text, Nave surveys the uses of the Greek terms translated as "repent" and "repentance"—*metanoia* and *metanoeo*—within the Greek-speaking world around the time of Jesus and the writing of the New Testament.

To summarize Nave's conclusions, he insists the claim "that there is little or no affinity between the usage of [*metanoeo*] and [*metanoia*] in non-Christian Greek literature and its usage in Christian literature" is wrong.[9] He outlines how "Christians undoubtedly developed some special nuances in their concept of repentance; however, there are clear continuities with the way the concept was used by philosophers, orators, and popular moralists in the world around them."[10] The common usage of the words in non-Christian Greek literature helps us understand the biblical usage of the words. The commonalities between Greek non-Christian and Christian usage of the verb *metanoeo* includes the idea of thinking differently or changing "one's mind or view, to form a different opinion, plan or purpose."[11] The noun *metanoia* within the Greek-speaking world came to mean "a change of mind, heart, view, opinion, or purpose."[12] With both words, Nave notes, "a sense of regret and or remorse is also implied."[13] Nave continues to show how these themes extend to the uses of the verb *metanoeo* and the noun *metanoia* within Greek-speaking Hebrew sources as well, coupled with the added component of conversion or "turning away from evil and ungodly behavior."[14]

Nave's observations on the use and common themes of *metanoeo* and *metanoia* within these different sources indicate scholars are well informed as to the definitions and uses of these words. Through his study, Nave also shows nuances do exist and different works and authors emphasize different aspects while using *metanoeo* and *metanoia*. A greater and fuller examination of the Hebrew and Greek words translated as "repent"/"repentance" or used to convey the concept of repentance is offered in chapter 4.

Returning to Nave's main objective, to examine repentance within Luke-Acts via a literary approach, he walks his reader through several of the narratives where "repent"/"repentance" is found. Throughout our study

---

9. Nave, *Repentance in Luke–Acts*, 40.

10. Nave, *Repentance in Luke–Acts*, 40.

11. Nave, *Repentance in Luke–Acts*, 69.

12. Nave, *Repentance in Luke–Acts*, 69.

13. Nave, *Repentance in Luke–Acts*, 69.

14. Nave, *Repentance in Luke–Acts*, 93, 116.

of repentance, we examine some of the same passages, however, from a different perspective. Throughout Nave's commentary on the repentance passages in Luke-Acts, he presents three distinctive ways repentance is used within these narratives. First, Nave suggests the words "repent" and "repentance" "essentially mean a change in thinking that usually leads to a change in behavior."[15] Secondly, he proposes, "Repentance in Luke-Acts represents a fundamental change in thinking that enables diverse individuals to receive the salvation of God and to live together as a community of God's people."[16] Thirdly, Nave says, "Repentance may represent an individual decision, but it often transforms social relationships."[17] Nave is absolutely correct here. Repentance is an individual choice but also much more. This idea becomes clearer as we continue through the upcoming pages.

As with Boda, Nave begins the conversation admirably but fails to note or connect the fact that while Luke[18] writes to give an account of the life of Jesus, he also writes his account within the context of the early church. Therefore, repentance is not just a focus of John the Baptist, Jesus, and the disciples, but of the early church as well.[19] This observation is vital to our present study. In what way was the message of repentance part of the message of the early church? And how did the message of repentance continue the work of God begun by John the Baptist and Jesus? It seems clear there is an aspect of repentance that relates to the church and its mission, and therefore to God's ultimate ends, needing our exploration.

REPENTANCE AS UNIVERSAL: MICHAEL J. OVEY

Also addressing Luke-Acts but from a completely different angle is Michael J. Ovey's work *The Feasts of Repentance: From Luke-Acts to Systematic and Pastoral Theology*. Within this work, Ovey looks specifically at the narratives of feasts or meals, including Luke 5:27–32; 7:36–50; 11:37–54; 14:1–24; 15; 19:1–10. Jesus came, Ovey acknowledges, to "save the lost and call sinners to repentance,"[20] and he sees this occur within the setting of meals in

15. Nave, *Repentance in Luke–Acts*, 145.

16. Nave, *Repentance in Luke–Acts*, 146.

17. Nave, *Repentance in Luke–Acts*, 158.

18. I will assume the traditional view that Luke wrote Luke-Acts.

19. Nave writes on this point, "The gospel story begins with John the Baptist preaching repentance during his period of ministry. After the period of John the Baptist ends, Jesus preaches repentance during his period of ministry, and after the period of Jesus ends, the disciples preach repentance during their period of ministry." Nave, *Repentance in Luke–Acts*, 194.

20. Ovey, *Feasts of Repentance*, 12.

Luke's gospel. These meal scenes show repentance is "universalizable" with the "apparently faithful character group, the Pharisees, and the apparently unfaithful character group, the tax collectors and sinners," who both must repent.[21] In Ovey's view, one place Luke addresses this theme of universal repentance is during meal scenes. Ovey admits "this does not exhaust Luke's repentance material and it examines the material from a particular perspective, but one that is consistent with Luke's aim of persuading readers as they see a sequence of characters responding to Jesus."[22]

The specifics of Ovey's exegesis are not our primary concern; rather we once again want to see where Ovey moves close to the target of our examination but falls just short. His task within the book is to "examine first the biblical material Luke-Acts affords, move to more systematic considerations and then to pastoral theology as we consider repentance in the corporate life of the people of God."[23] When coming to this section, however, Ovey focuses on how repentance affects the people of God relationally as individuals. When Ovey turns to address the systematic and pastoral aspects of his study, he is close to asking the right question: "Does the repentance of the individual impact our corporate life before the return of Jesus Christ, and what shape does repentance give to Christian life together after the individual comes to faith and repents?"[24] We can see the similarity between Ovey's questions and Nave's earlier observation. They are both seeking to connect repentance to something bigger; however, Ovey's answers, like Nave's, while certainly true, are not complete. Repentance does allow Christians to be relationally connected by removing self-righteousness, pride, and hypocrisy, and bringing humility.[25] But is that all? Beyond the individual aspects, repentance has a role within the ecclesiastical community of the church. If that is true, then repentance stands as part of the mission of the church and therefore an aspect of the mission of God.

CONCLUSION

These three authors have offered helpful studies of repentance covering biblical, literary, and systematic theologies. Additionally, each offers a launching point for our current discussion of repentance. Each comes close to making the connections this work makes, though none of them takes the next step.

21. Ovey, *Feasts of Repentance*, 8–9.

22. Ovey, *Feasts of Repentance*, 11.

23. Ovey, *Feasts of Repentance*, 6.

24. Ovey, *Feasts of Repentance*, 133.

25. We will explore some of these themes in chapter 7.

Throughout the upcoming pages this study addresses those shortcomings and takes the next step. This work develops an understanding of repentance that matters to the church, becomes a part of the mission of the church, and points toward God's ultimate ends. We see how repentance makes us into the people of God, places us within God's mission in the world, and leads us to live in the reality that Jesus reigns as King over his people.

Let's begin by asking the question: what is God's mission? What is God doing?

2

What Is God Doing?

THE BEST COMPANIES HAVE powerful and compelling mission statements. Ford Motor Company proclaims, "We are here for one purpose, to help build a better world, where every person is free to move and pursue their dreams."[1] Nike aspires "to move the world forward" by "building community, protecting our planet, and increasing access to sport."[2] A mission statement tells the purpose of the company, and a well-articulated mission statement can define success or failure. It answers the question: what should this company be focusing on?

How many of us have asked a similar question of the church or of God? We have wondered, what defines success for the church? Or what is God's mission in the world? The first time I heard those questions being asked was in the early 2000s. I was hearing these questions being asked within the writings surrounding the emergent and missional church.[3] From my perspective as a young adult who grew up attending traditional, conservative evangelical churches and who felt called into ministry, these writings were exciting. Someone was thinking about the changes in culture and how believers within the community of the church could not only respond, but thrive. They were asking questions that seemed important; questions about the mission of the church: what should the church be doing? And they were

1. Ford Motor Company, "Our Purpose," paragraph 1.

2. Nike, "Impact: Taking Action," paragraph 1.

3. Our purpose is not to be detoured by the emergent or missional discussion. It is simply the context where I first heard questions of purpose and mission being asked.

asking questions about the mission of God: what has God done and what is God doing in the world?

These are still important questions I have returned to ponder throughout the years that have followed. The answer to these questions doesn't seem to be having more people in the seats or more money in the offering. I believe what God is doing in the world is what God has *always* been doing in the world—calling people to turn to him. If this is what God is doing, then it follows it should be what his followers ought to be doing as well.

The belief that we, as followers of God, should be about continuing the work of God surely is not new to pastors or many Christians. We know Jesus' commissions in Matthew 28:19–20 and Acts 1:8. We've heard about going and making disciples. We've heard about being witnesses of Jesus when the Holy Spirit empowers us. We have heard those messages, and we have taken them seriously. They have produced missionary movements and organizations, ways of sharing the Christian faith with others, and have helped bring millions of people to Christ. However, over the last twenty years, at least, the constant refrain from researchers in the West has been the decline in church attendance and in new believers (often represented by baptisms).[4] What's the source for this disconnect? We have neglected another of Jesus' commissions, this one found in Luke 24:45–48:

> Now He said to them, "These are My words which I spoke to you while I was still with you, that all things which are written about Me in the Law of Moses and the Prophets and the Psalms must be fulfilled." Then He opened their minds to understand the Scriptures, and He said to them, "Thus it is written, that the Christ would suffer and rise again from the dead the third day, and that repentance for forgiveness of sins would be proclaimed in His name to all the nations, beginning from Jerusalem.

Recapturing the biblical call to repentance and seeing it as a central piece of God's mission in the world and therefore the mission of the church in the world can be the way the message of Jesus Christ can connect to the culture once again.

Despite all of our good intentions to carry out the Great Commission and be witnesses for Jesus Christ in the world, and call men and women to salvation, could it be we are seeing the rotten fruits of raising generations of Christians with an impoverished sense of repentance? Could it be we have generations of men and women who called themselves Christians but who have never been taught what it means to turn to God? Or, to use

4. See Jones, "U.S. Church Membership;" Pew Research Center, "Decline of Christianity;" Shellnutt, "Biggest Drop in 100 Years."

John the Baptist's words and ask it another way, are we failing to see and hear the fruits of repentance in the lives of believers? I believe this is indeed what we are seeing in the church and among Christians today. It has been over a decade since Barna research reported, "in virtually every study we conduct . . . born-again Christians fail to display much attitudinal or behavioral evidence of transformed lives . . . we found that most of the lifestyle activities of born-again Christians were statistically equivalent to those of non-born-agains."[5]

Now, in the early part of the 2020s, we find more Americans deriving their identity from their politics than from their faith. This has led to individuals associating certain religious groups with certain political ideologies.[6] We have more self-proclaimed Christians finding truth on Facebook than truth in the words of Scripture. And what Pete Philips, director of the Codec Research Centre for Digital Theology at Durham University, observed in the UK in 2017 is certainly true of many in the American church today. He says, "A lot of people who consider themselves to be active Christians may not strictly even believe in God or Jesus or the acts described in the Bible . . . A new kind of mutated Christianity for a digital age is appearing, one that follows many of the ethics of the secular world."[7]

The issues noted above transcend the political left, right, and center. They transcend born-again or nominal Christians, and span across denominations. They are united by believing the only place we can turn for truth is ourselves. The individual is the only one who can decide what is true to that individual. Not only that, the individual is the only one who can define reality for that individual. Everything, then, including religion becomes egocentric. God becomes beholden to me and what I need for a full and flourishing life is not to turn to God, but rather for God to acquiesce and meet my needs. In many ways this has become the message of the evangelical church in America today. The mission of the church has become a mission to make "Christians" who have all their consumer, emotional, and relational needs met by God, instead of a mission of repentance, where men and women turn to God, enter into the kingdom, find forgiveness of sins, and become the people of God. If we, as Christians, want to stand out from the culture, grow in Christian maturity, and bear fruit; if we want the church to be vibrant, living, and world changing; if we want to invite a world into

---

5. Kinnaman and Lyons, *Unchristian*, 47. Kinnaman and Lyons define a "born-again Christian" as an individual who "has made a personal commitment to Jesus Christ that is still important to the person and if he or she has confessed sins and accepted Jesus Christ as his or her Savior." *Unchristian*, 252.

6. See Smith, "More White Americans."

7. Stokel-Walker, "How Smartphones and Social Media," paragraphs 15–16.

a different way of life, it will take a rediscovering of repentance. It will take a rediscovery of both the fullness of repentance, as seen within the Bible, as well as repentance as a central piece of the mission of God and the mission of the church. That is the purpose of this work and our mission going forward.

Exploring and defining repentance specifically is found in chapter 4; however, at this point a working definition is needed to understand why I'm making this claim. The basic idea of repentance is a turning, a turning from one position to another position, or a turning from one state of being to another state of being. As Christians we should be calling those in the world to turn to God. Such a message is not just a message for Christians or a message for the church; it is the very message of God to us. The way God will bring human beings to turn back to him is a central, but neglected, aspect of both the Old Testament and New Testament. Thus, this chapter and the following chapter of this volume survey both testaments to demonstrate one crucial aspect of God's mission is turning or returning. This includes both God's people turning/returning to him and God turning/returning to his people. The next chapter shows how Jesus continues this emphasis within his mission and ministry.

What is God doing? It is to this question we turn as a launching-off point for the main emphasis of this work.

WHAT IS GOD DOING?

The mission of God stands as the natural place to begin exploring the theme of repentance. Why begin with God's mission? All good theology begins with God. Whether we want to know God's character and attributes or understand our relationship and position relative to God, the starting place is God himself. As Christians within the context of the church, we may ask what our mission is. This is the topic of a later chapter, but as we lay a foundation, we must first ask: what is the mission of God? What is God doing? We must understand this before we can understand our part within it and, as the theme of this work, where the doctrine of repentance fits within the mission of God and within our mission as the church.

My starting point to understanding God's mission is the Bible. Christopher J. H. Wright introduces his work on the mission of God by stating, "Mission is what the Bible is all about; we could as meaningfully talk of the missional basis of the Bible as of the biblical basis of mission."[8] Wright is not merely undertaking word gymnastics here. His point, and the point of

8. C. J. H. Wright, *Mission of God*, 29.

his work *The Mission of God,* states the truth that we understand mission from the Bible and the Bible is understood as missional.[9] The very fact we have the Bible, the Word of God given to us through human authors by the inspiration of the Holy Spirit, to be God's self-revelation is itself missional. It reveals to us some of what God has been and is doing. It reveals God's mission to us. As we seek to define God's mission through the Bible, what do we find?

The mission of God, what has often been called the *missio Dei,* includes God's creation of the world, his actions within the world, and his plans and purposes for the world. This is the singular painting the whole biblical narrative helps to fashion. The entirety of the Bible, through its different writers and types of literature, utilizes different colors, offers shading and contrast, and emphasizes different angles, but all contribute to this one painting. Additionally, some biblical texts contribute to the background and others to the foreground, nevertheless the picture created through the Bible reveals the mission of God. Good art does more than just capture a moment in time; it tells a story. The same is true for the painting composed by the biblical writers. The *missio Dei* has been defined simply as "the story of God's love for and relationship with his creation."[10] As this story is fleshed out, more details become clear:

> The story reveals that God is the only God, the only One who creates, and that he creates all things good. . .Covenant love is sent to God's creation with blessings for fidelity and curses for neglect. Humanity refuses to be faithful, refuses to honor God as God, and so it suffers the loss of relationship, purity, and place. Cast out of God's immediate presence, humanity is reminded of God's love through the law, and yet the ongoing story is of humanity's rejection of God and search for other gods, including the god of self. Most of the scriptural story is about humanity's disobedience, God's call to return, God's sending of messengers (judges, kings, prophets), and finally God's sending of his own Son to fulfill covenant love.[11]

Describing the same picture of the *missio Dei,* however, from a slightly different viewpoint, helps us understand the way the biblical narrative answers what Christopher Wright suggests are the "four fundamental worldview questions that all religions and philosophies answer in one way or

---

9. C. J. H. Wright, *Mission of God,* 33. Wright calls this a "missional hermeneutic." *Mission of God,* 33. Also see Sunquist, *Understanding Christian Mission,* 180.

10. Sunquist, *Understanding Christian Mission,* 181.

11. Sunquist, *Understanding Christian Mission,* 182.

another."[12] The four questions are: Where are we? Who are we? What's gone wrong? What is the solution?[13] The story of God as we begin to see it unfold in the Old Testament, as his mission to the world, answers these questions. We live on the earth, the habitat created by "the one living, personal God."[14] We are beings made by God, in his image and likeness, and given a unique spiritual and moral position among God's creation. The wrong we see within what was once God's good and perfect creation is the result of humankind's "rebellion and disobedience against our Creator God."[15] The solution to this problem resides with God alone and God has initiated it "through his choice and creation of a people, Israel, through whom God intends eventually to bring blessings to all nations of the earth and ultimately to renew the whole creation."[16]

These two concise summaries of the biblical story disclose one of the aspects of God's mission comprising our focus: returning. The first act of God the Bible records is the creation of the world in Genesis 1. Within each step of creation, at the close of each day, God declares his work *tov*, "good," including humanity, whom he describes as "very good." As we have been reminded of in these summaries, humanity's disobedience, idolatry, pride, and rebellion brought sin, evil, and brokenness into God's good world. As a result, human beings have separated themselves from God. God's plan to have a people for himself, however, was not thwarted forever. He would make a way to return; God would return his creation to its pre-fallen state and God would make a way for his human creations, those created in his image and likeness, to return to him as well. Thus, "the Bible is a love story, the story of a loving God who will not let go and watch his people reap their own destruction. He is constantly sending (*missio*), reminding, calling, forgiving, and judging."[17] God is also returning and calling his people to return. In that calling, we find the mission of repentance.

THE MISSION OF RETURNING

God's action in the world, as we have just briefly explored, begins at creation. God creates human beings in his image and likeness, and in Genesis 2 the author zooms in to focus on and look at the creation of humanity as if

12. C. J. H. Wright, *Mission of God*, 55.

13. C. J. H. Wright, *Mission of God*, 55.

14. C. J. H. Wright, *Mission of God*, 55.

15. C. J. H. Wright, *Mission of God*, 55.

16. C. J. H. Wright, *Mission of God*, 55.

17. Sunquist, *Understanding Christian Mission*, 183.

under a microscope. As the focus narrows onto this being created in the image and likeness of God, we are drawn to search for clues as to the meaning of those words. In the Genesis 2 story, God forms Adam from the dust of the ground and "breathed into his nostrils the breath of life; and man became a living being" (Gen 2:7). The man is formed from both the ground and from the breath of God. The man is not God, because he was formed from the ground; but the man also contains the very breath of God. Thus, humanity has a dual origin story. While the breath of God is applied to all creatures in Psalm 104, within Genesis 2 it is uniquely given to human beings as a way of showing their distinction among the rest of creation.

Humans are set as stewards over God's creation, as the physical image of God in the world.[18] Within the perfect environment of the garden, humans and God lived in perfect fellowship, love, and union. And not only humans with God, but humans with creation and humans with each other. The capacity of human beings to have relationships, especially with God, is one of the facets of humanity being made in the image and likeness of God. Gregory of Nyssa speaks directly to this, as Nonna Verna Harrison summarizes: "Gregory shows how the image of God in which we are made is what enables us to be in relationship with God and grow in that relationship. The divine image makes possible the participation in the life and goodness of God."[19]

Until Genesis 3.

When Adam and Eve disobeyed, they attempted to no longer be merely beings created by God and instead desired to become like God himself—which included having God's knowledge of good and evil (Gen 3:5). They disregarded God's command to refrain from eating from the tree of knowledge of good and evil and thereby sinned against God. We commonly call this episode "the fall," meaning the beginning of sin on earth and within human beings, resulting in a falling away from God and from the state of perfection that characterized God's creation. If we want to be true in describing the painting the biblical writers are composing in all its fullness, seeing this event as *the turn* gives us another way to understand the story the picture is telling. This scene points to a turn away from God and toward sin. We speak more of sin in a later chapter.

For our purpose here, however, our focus is on God's address to each party—the serpent, Eve, and Adam—as recorded in Genesis 3:14–19, after the sin occurs. In these verses God pronounces judgment, or perhaps we might say he declares the consequences of their actions. The way we

---

18. See McKnight, *Community Called Atonement*, 19, 21.

19. Harrison, *God's Many-Splendored Image*, 33.

understand these verses is extremely important. Judgment implies God's response to their sin is complete—they sinned, God judged, the result stands. The prior paradigm has been changed by God's action, not the action of sin. Consequences acknowledge something has changed because of the action that has taken place. The paradigm has changed because of the sin committed. Therefore, the issue that must be dealt with is the issue of sin. This sets the stage for God's mission in the world beginning in Genesis 3 and continuing throughout the Bible.

God's words highlight the breakdown within each of the relationships we mentioned earlier. Humanity's relationship with creation is broken: there will be hostility between the serpent and humans and the ground, from which all plants and animals were created, is now cursed. The relationship of humanity with each other is broken, as men will now seek to rule over women and women will find that pain will now accompany their role in God's command to multiply and fill the earth.

Not only this, but humanity's relationship with God is also broken. We see this in Genesis 3:19:

> By the sweat of your face
> You will eat bread,
> Till you return to the ground,
> Because from it you were taken;
> For you are dust,
> And to dust you shall return.

The key section for our exploration is the second half of God's words, "Till you return to the ground, because from it you were taken; for you are dust and to dust you shall return." Because of the sin of Adam and Eve, humanity stands separated from God and the destiny of every human being is to return, or turn, to the ground. Instead of returning to God, our end will be a return to the ground. Human beings were taken from the ground and made into living creatures, created to be in eternal relationship with a spiritual God. After the turn in Genesis 3, our destiny is not an eternity in God's presence, as in Revelation 21, but rather a returning or turning to the ground.

The God-breathed part of us (we may call it our "heart" or our "soul"), however, longs to return to God. The great mission of God, as told in the Bible, is that God also desires our return to him. This mission unites the narrative of the whole Bible.[20] God's initial purpose for creating human beings in the first place—to have a covenant people—is not thwarted but rather becomes the central focus of God's mission. God will move to bless the world by calling a man, then a family, then a nation, then the nations to

20. Köstenberger and Alexander, *Salvation of the Ends of the Earth*, 11.

turn/return to him as the one true God. The mission of God is a mission of turning, a mission of repentance.

Mark J. Boda, however, argues that repentance "does not play a dominant role" within the story of Genesis.[21] He admits the narratives highlight sin; "however repentance does not play a role, although there are warnings and treatments of the shame and consequences of sin, all highlighting the crisis of the human condition and the need for avenues of renewal for the relationship between God, humanity, and creation."[22] While Boda is correct in saying repentance is not a major theme in terms of individuals turning away from specific sins and turning toward God, it is a major theme in what God does to address the turning from him that is both the cause and effect of sin. Genesis introduces the problem of sin, as Boda affirms, but it also introduces the solution—a turning/returning to God, initiated by God in the calling of Abraham and promised to all of creation through Abraham's descendants.

This is God's mission, the *missio Dei*; this is what God is doing throughout the Bible and, as will become clear as we progress, it is still what God is doing. We do, in fact, see this theme in Genesis and throughout the Old Testament. Let us now turn our attention to surveying this theme in several important Old Testament passages, beginning with Abraham, Isaac, and Jacob and the theme of returning to the promised land.

A COVENANT AND LAND OF RETURNING

In Genesis 12:1, God calls out to Abram to "go forth" from his home and his relatives to the land God will show him. Within God's calling of Abram are promises. These promises are fourfold and consist of the "promise of land, descendants, covenant, and blessing to the nations."[23] We read:

> Now the Lord said to Abram,
> "Go forth from your country,
> And from your relatives
> And from your father's house,
> To the land which I will show you;

21. Boda, "Renewal," 3.

22. Boda, "Renewal," 3–4.

23. Wenham, *Genesis 1–15*, 268. Also see Gooder, *Pentateuch*. Gooder highlights three promises: "the promise of descendants ('I will make of you a great nation'); the promise of relationship with God ('I will bless you, and make your name great') and the promise of land ('Go from your country. . .to the land that I will show you')." *Pentateuch*, 57–58.

> And I will make you a great nation,
> And I will bless you,
> And make your name great;
> And so you shall be a blessing;
> And I will bless those who bless you,
> And the one who curses you I will curse.
> And in you all the families of the earth will be blessed. (Gen 12:1–3)

Within this passage we find that "God's mission of world redemption begins."[24] This is the way God will make a people for himself, a people who will return to him and turn toward him. Within this covenant pronouncement and the subsequent retellings of the covenant (Gen 13:14–17; 15:1–21; 17:1–9; 22:15–18), all but one mention the promise of land and each one speaks of Abram's (Abraham's) relationship to the nations and that through him God's purpose for the nations will be completed. We are meant to see a connection between the promise of a land and God's action of blessing all the nations. As Abram travels, he comes to the land of Canaan and God tells him, "To your descendants I will give this land" (Gen 12:7), thus equating the land of Canaan to the promised land. As the narrative progresses from Abraham, to Isaac, and especially to Jacob, the promise of the land, and a returning to the land, becomes a central theme.

As we follow the story of Abraham, he obeys God and travels to the land of Canaan, where God declares this is the land promised to Abraham and his descendants. At this point, a fair question to ask is: why is the promise of land important? One proposal is that God's fourfold promise to Abraham represents "what he intended for the whole human race at the beginning."[25] The promised land represents a new garden of Eden, a place where God's people can live as God's people, and where they can rely on God to meet their needs, "including land, food and fellowship."[26] The land, therefore, stands as a tangible symbol of God's covenant. God will call a people back to him and the land is a symbol showing that human beings can return to God, as God's people, through God's covenant promise.

With Abraham's grandson, Jacob, the return to the land and through the return to the land, a return to God becomes an even greater theme. The life of Jacob spans the biblical narrative from Genesis 25 to Genesis 50, with Joseph's story taking center stage beginning in chapter 37. We obviously cannot retell all of Jacob's story; rather I shall point out the sections

24. C. J. H. Wright, *Mission of God*, 200.

25. Wenham, *Exploring the Old Testament*, 41.

26. Wenham, *Exploring the Old Testament*, 41.

where the return to the land is seen. Among the commonalities between these texts, in addition to God's promise and call to Jacob to return, is the Hebrew word for "turn" or "return," *shub*, used in each text. We explore this word in greater detail in chapter 4. The important point to note here is when God repeats the covenant promises to Jacob, it comes by way of a return to the land.

In Genesis 28 Jacob flees from Esau; as he travels, he stops to sleep and God comes to Jacob in a dream and tells him, in part, "Behold, I am with you and will keep you wherever you go, and will bring you back (return you, turn you back) to this land; for I will not leave you until I have done what I have promised you" (28:15). This promise comes within the context of God choosing Jacob's line as the one through whom God's promise of redemption will come. God identifies himself as the God of Abraham and Isaac (28:13), and the promise of descendants and universal blessing God makes to Jacob is obviously an echo to the promise made to Abraham (28:14). This is a repeating of the covenant made to Abraham, and the promise of land (28:13) and the promise to return to the land (28:15) bookend the covenant promises.

In Genesis 31, after Jacob has married and gained flocks from his father-in-law, Laban, God again addresses Jacob, "Then the Lord said to Jacob, 'Return to the land of your fathers and to your relatives, and I will be with you" (31:3). As Jacob returns, he encounters God (32:24–32).

As the Joseph story unfolds, it explains how Jacob's family arrives in Egypt. While God is certainly with Joseph and orchestrates his rise to power within Egypt, there is still a sense as the Genesis narrative closes that something is missing because the people are not in the land of promise. This underscores some of Jacob's final words in Genesis 48:21, "Then Israel (Jacob) said to Joseph, 'Behold, I am about to die, but God will be with you, and bring you back to the land of your fathers.'" Here Jacob extends the promise of God to his sons, especially Joseph.

When Jacob dies, Joseph returns to Canaan to bury Jacob but, "After he had buried his father, Joseph returned to Egypt, he and brothers, and all who had gone up with him to bury his father" (50:14). As the Genesis narrative closes, the descendants of Abraham have not returned to the promised land; instead they have returned to Egypt.

What I have argued in this section is the concept we later designate as "repentance" does, in fact, play a role within the narratives.[27] As God calls to humanity to return to him, it is as the people of God, a nation called

---

27. Also see Boda, *Return to* Me, 35–36. However, I have argued the entire calling of Abraham and God's covenant with him and his descendants also focuses on the theme of repentance.

out from the nations, with a land—a new Eden—where the people of God could live reliant upon him. The promise to return to the land thus, as we've outlined, becomes a central component and a form of shorthand for the entire work of God.

SIN AS TURNING AWAY

Before we return to tracing the theme of turning/returning as part of God's mission within the Old Testament, a slight detour is needed to feature how the Old Testament pictures sin as a turning from God. This background will assist us in chapter 4 when we move to define repentance. As we saw in examining Adam and Eve above, sin brings God's judgment and results in consequences that separate human beings from God. Scot McKnight engages in a beneficial summary when he defines sin as "distortion in all directions—toward God, self, others, and world."[28] He notes that throughout the Old Testament several metaphors or terms are used for sin. He asks: "Is it rebellion (*pesha*)? Infidelity (*meshubah*)? Disloyalty (*beged*)? Getting dirty (*tum'ah*)? Wandering (*'avon*)? Trespass (*ma'al*)? Transgression (*'abar*)? Failure or missing the mark (*chatta't*)?"[29] Missing from McKnight's otherwise exhaustive list is turning (*shub* or *sûr*).[30]

Within the Old Testament sin is described as turning from God's commands. Several examples are seen in Deuteronomy.[31] A key—some would say the key—passage in Deuteronomy is found in chapter 4.[32] This passage also directly relates back to our previous discussion of the land within the covenant promise. Deuteronomy itself is a series of addresses by Moses near the end of his life. The opening address, chapters 1–4, recounts the history of the people, beginning with the giving of the law at Mt. Sinai (Horeb) and ending with foretelling of Israel's sin by forgetting the covenant and serving other gods.[33] While I encourage the reader to read the passage in whole, I note here only the beginning and the middle of Deuteronomy 4, verses 1–2 and 30–31:

---

28. McKnight, *Community Called Atonement*, 46.

29. McKnight, *Community Called Atonement*, 46.

30. Within the Old Testament, both the Hebrew words *shub* and *sûr* are translated as "turn" or "return."

31. Boda, "Renewal." Boda comments, "The book of Deuteronomy has long been recognized as the key locus for penitential theology in the Torah." "Renewal," 7.

32. See Boda, "Renewal," 7.

33. See C. J. H. Wright, *Mission of God*, 375–87.

> "Now, O Israel, listen to the statutes and the judgments which I am teaching you to perform, so that you may live and go in and take possession of the land which the Lord, the God of your fathers, is giving you. You shall not add to the word which I am commanding you, nor take away from it, that you may keep the commandments of the Lord your God which I command you …When you are in distress and all these things have come upon you, in the latter days you will return to the Lord your God and listen to His voice. For the Lord your God is a compassionate God; He will not fail you nor destroy you nor forget the covenant with your fathers which He swore to them."

In these verses we find a connection between the covenant at Sinai and the covenant to Abraham and a definition of sin as turning away from God. Instead of a direct definition (i.e., sin is turning from God), what we find is an indirect definition. If forgetting God's covenant and serving idols requires a return, a turning back, to the Lord, then the actions that are "evil in the sight of the Lord your God" and will "provoke [God] to anger" (4:25) constitute a turning away.[34] This connection continues in Deuteronomy 30:1–10:

> So it shall be when all of these things have come upon you, the blessing and the curse which I have set before you, and you call them to mind in all the nations where the Lord your God has banished you, and you return to the Lord your God and obey Him with all your heart and soul according to all that I command you today, you and your sons, then the Lord your God will restore you from captivity, and have compassion on you, and will gather you again from all the peoples where the Lord your God has scattered you. If your outcasts are at the ends of the earth, from there the Lord your God will gather you, and from there He will bring you back. The Lord your God will bring you into the land which your fathers possessed, and you shall possess it; and He will prosper you and multiply you more than your fathers. Moreover the Lord your God will circumcise your heart and the heart of your descendants, to love the Lord your God with all your heart and with all your soul, so that you may live. The Lord your God will inflict all these curses on your enemies and on those who hate you, who persecuted you. And you shall again obey the Lord, and observe all His commandments which I command you today. Then the Lord your God will prosper you abundantly in all the work of your hand, in the

---

34. The Hebrew word used in this passage is *shub*.

> offspring of your body and the offspring of your cattle and in
> the produce of your ground, for the Lord will again rejoice over
> you for good, just as He rejoiced over your fathers; if you obey
> the Lord your God to keep His commandments and His statutes
> which are written in this book of the law, if you turn to the Lord
> your God with all your heart and soul.

Here the returning from exile, the turning to God, and the return to the land converge. If returning means obedience to God with all one's "heart and soul," then turning away means a turning away from God in one's heart and soul. We also see turning to God is a turning *within* our heart and soul. We find similar calls to return to the Lord after committing evil and serving other gods. Additionally, we read directives to remain true to God's commands by not turning away from them; thus turning would be to commit sin against God. We find instances of this in Deuteronomy 17:11, 20; 28:14; 31:29.[35]

While turning from God is not the only definition or metaphor used for sin within the Old Testament, the writer of Deuteronomy certainly understands sin as doing what is evil in the sight of the Lord, forgetting the covenant, and serving other gods—in short, turning away from God. The solution to this turning away, however, is a return. Let's look at this aspect of turning now.

GOD'S CALL TO RETURN

We've already seen how God's mission is to make a way for returning by calling a people, beginning with Abraham and extending to all the nations. Central to this covenant was a land of promise, a land given by God to his people where they would live in relationship with him—in the new Eden— where they would know God and be the people of God. God's people would be, the prophets preach, a light to the nations and draw them to turn to God (Isa 51:4; 60). Christopher Wright affirms this from the text of Deuteronomy 4, examined above. He summarizes the passage, saying, "The whole chapter, then, is a microcosm of Deuteronomy as a whole. It is an urgent call to covenant loyalty through exclusive worship of YHWH alone, based on the unique history of his redeeming and revealing activity through the Exodus and Sinai, and worked out in practical and ethical obedience to his laws in the land of promise, *with a view to the affect this will have on the nations*" (emphasis added).[36] The prophecy or foreshadowing of Moses in

35. These verses all contain the Hebrew word *sur* for "return."

36. C. J. H. Wright, *Mission of God*, 377.

Deuteronomy, however, comes to pass. The nation of Israel, the people of God, break the covenant, forget their love relationship with God, and worship false gods. They need to return to God just as much as the nations.

The failure of Israel to live by God's commands and covenant as God's people show us two important truths about turning to God. First, there is tension present between God's choosing the nation of Israel as his people and the acknowledgment that not all in Israel have chosen to live as the people of God. Jesus makes this distinction clear within his ministry. Within the Old Testament we find this distinction when the text says individuals or generations did not know the Lord (Judg 2:10; 1 Sam 2:12; Jer 2:8). Second, to truly be the people of God, even those within Israel who turned away to sin must turn back to God. This is central to the *missio Dei*. Let's consider examples.

We cannot look at every one of the references to turning or returning in the Old Testament. There are over one thousand uses of the Hebrew word *shub* alone.[37] Instead, I want to note two key texts found in the words of the prophet Ezekiel. Many times, the words of the prophets come to mind when we think about God's appeal for his people to turn away from their sins and return to him. The messages of the prophets "show that the God of creation, the Lord of history remains faithful to love and to covenant despite the people's infidelities, transgressions, and impenitence. Throughout the prophetic texts we see the role the heart plays in relation to repentance, fidelity, reconciliation, and transformation."[38]

Ezekiel preached to the people of Israel as they were exiled in Babylon. He was both a priest and a prophet, and "proclaimed to the exiled Jews in Babylonia the Lord's judgment and ultimate blessing."[39] Many of Ezekiel's messages are pronouncements of sin and its consequences; however, there are also notes of restoration and renewal. Ezekiel's message to the exiled nation is a message of the faithfulness of God; God fulfills his "promises both to judge and to bless."[40] Yet even now God's judgment has come: "the Lord desired to turn the exiles of Israel away from their sinful ways and restore them to himself."[41] Thus, even as God's promise of restoration does not negate the seriousness of sin, Ezekiel's message is one of turning/returning to God.[42]

---

37. Nave, *Role and Function of Repentance*, 112.

38. Dempsey, "'Turn Back,'" 47.

39. Alexander, *Ezekiel*, 739.

40. Alexander, *Ezekiel*, 743.

41. Alexander, *Ezekiel*, 743.

42. Boda notes the most common Hebrew word that connotes turning, returning,

In Ezekiel 14, we read an oracle of the prophet against the elders of Israel. Within the message, Ezekiel denounces setting up idols within the heart, which God declares is iniquity that estranges the one who commits the iniquity from him. Then God, through Ezekiel, calls for turning and pronounces judgment for those who do not return:

> Therefore say to the house of Israel, "Thus says the Lord God, 'Repent and turn away from your idols and turn your faces away from all your abominations. For anyone of the house of Israel or of the immigrants who stay in Israel who separates himself from Me, sets up his idols in his heart, puts right before his face the stumbling block of his iniquity, and then comes to the prophet to inquire of Me for himself, I the Lord will be brought to answer him in My own person. I will set My face against that man and make him a sign and a proverb, and I will cut him off from among My people. So you will know that I am the Lord." (Ezek 14:6–8)

While Ezekiel's message is preached directly to the elders of Israel, this call to repent or turn is directed at the entire nation.[43] The entire nation had replaced God—the God of Abraham, Isaac, and Jacob—with imaginary and false idols. Even if, at the time Ezekiel preached, worship of God at the temple was still occurring, the people had set idols in their hearts and "in the final analysis, anything, whether good or bad in and of itself, becomes an idol whenever it is allowed to compromise one's loyalty to God."[44] Therefore God declares the whole nation should turn from their idols and turn their faces from their sins and the implication is that turning from idols means turning toward God. If anyone does not turn from his idolatry and return to God, the consequence will be that God will "cut him off" from his people—not cut off from God, but not counted among those who have together turned toward God in repentance and who will then be restored by him to the fullness of life.

We are confronted here with God's call to turn to him. The call to return is set within the judgment of idolatry. Turning in Ezekiel "always involves turning away from an evil practice."[45] The worship of other gods, even within one's heart, constitutes a turning away from God and necessitates a returning to him. The emphasis on the heart and the face in the passage "highlights the internal (heart) and external (face) nature of

---

or repenting in Ezekiel is *shub*. Boda, *Return to Me*, 88.

43. Brownlee, *Ezekiel 1–19*, 205.

44. Brownlee, *Ezekiel 1–19*, 205.

45. Boda, *Return to Me*, 88.

repentance."[46] A failure to accept God's invitation to turn back to him is paramount to removal from the people of God. However, Ezekiel's message is not only directed to the elders and the nation of Israel; it also includes the "immigrants" or "resident alien" (14:7). The inclusion of non-Israelites within the call to turn to God shows even "the alien who adheres to the worship of the Lord alone belongs to His people and with them may share in His worship."[47]

The second passage we examine in Ezekiel where we find God calling on his people to return to him is found in chapter 18. Ezekiel 33 contains "echoes" of Ezekiel 18; therefore it is helpful to reference both passages here.[48] Walter Brueggemann says three categories of sin are described within Ezekiel 18: idolatry, "distorted sexuality," and "distorted economics."[49] Brueggemann sees that these three categories of sin "[preclude] Ezekiel's listeners from limiting their horizon of sin, alienation, and confession to their preferred sin."[50] Brueggemann reminds us here the sins God emphasizes, denounces, and commands turning from are defined by God and express the opposite of the character of God. God tells us what causes us to turn away from him, and it's God who then calls us and gives us an opportunity to return.

The "accent" within Ezekiel 18 is found, according to Brueggemann, in the five imperatives.[51] These are found in 18:30 ("repent" and "turn away"), 18:31 ("cast away" and "make"), and 18:32 ("repent"). Of these five commands, three are tied to turning.[52] The commands by God to turn to him are not the only times turning is mentioned in Ezekiel 18. Before God gives the imperatives to turn, we find four instances where sin is described as turning away from righteousness (Ezek 18:24, 25, 26,). Directly prior to these statements, God says in 18:21, 22–23:

> "But if the wicked man turns from all his sins which he has committed and observes all My statutes and practices justice and righteousness, he shall surely live; he shall not die . . . Do I have any pleasure in the death of the wicked," declares the Lord God, "rather than that he should turn from his ways and live?"

46. Boda, *Return to Me*, 89.

47. Brownlee, *Ezekiel 1–19*, 203.

48. Boda, *Return to Me*, 90.

49. Brueggemann, "Summons," 367–68.

50. Brueggemann, "Summons," 368.

51. Brueggemann, "Summons," 368.

52. Each verb is a form of the Hebrew word *shub*.

We find other calls to turn from wickedness in 18:27 and 18:28. These verses assist in forming the connection between Ezekiel 18 and Ezekiel 33. There God repeats the emphasis found in Ezekiel 18, saying he takes no pleasure in the death of the wicked and implores Israel to "turn back, turn back from your evil ways" (33:11). In both passages the promise of God is turning back to him results in life, not death: "Therefore, repent and live" (18:32) and "'As I live!' declares the Lord God, 'I take no pleasure in the death of the wicked, but rather that the wicked turn from his way and live'" (33:11). God makes himself very clear: turning away from him, turning away from righteousness, and turning toward iniquity results in death, just as we saw all the way back in Genesis 3. In both passages, God declares he is right and just in his pronouncement that iniquity brings forth death (18:25–29, 33:17, 33:20). Turning to God, however, brings life and God will not remember the sin anymore (18:22, 33:16).

Within these passages in Ezekiel, we find multiple examples of the truths we have been exploring within this chapter: 1) God declares that sin is turning away from him and his righteousness and 2) God calls his people and all people (14:7) to turn back to him. This turning brings about 3) the forgiveness of sins; God will not remember them anymore; 4) those who repent will live; and 5) they will be the people of God. Ezekiel is merely one example of the turning/returning theme that we find, to a greater or lesser degree, in a number of the Old Testament prophets. Boda emphasizes "the Former and Latter Prophets [provide] the most extensive material for the theology of repentance in the Old Testament."[53] More examples of turning within the prophets are found in chapter 4.

THE GOD WHO TURNS

As we close this chapter, we would be remiss to not recognize that as God desires for his people to turn away from sin and return to him, he also desires to turn toward his people. Of course, this turning plays a huge role in the incarnation and the coming of Jesus, which we explore in the next chapter. It is, however, seen within the text of the Old Testament as well. As before, we cannot examine every text, for that would be a book in itself. Rather, I wish to point out and comment on two select passages from another Old Testament prophet—Isaiah.

The work of Isaiah contains some of the most well-known verses in all the Old Testament. Scarcely can a Christmas or Easter season go by without the familiar words of Isaiah being read as pointing the way to Jesus' coming

53. Boda, *Return to Me*, 107.

and Jesus' suffering. Isaiah, however, wrote primarily for his own generation and his messages are meant to "affect them, shake them, motivate them by confronting them with transcendental issues."[54] These transcendental issues include the holiness of God, the reality of sin, God's judgment, God's restoration, and God's work of salvation. Out of these issues, Isaiah calls both individuals and the nation of Israel to repentance. We see an example of this within the opening chapter. As the words of Isaiah begin, in what Geoffrey W. Grogan calls a summing of "the teaching, not only of Isaiah, but of the whole prophetic movement,"[55] God addresses the sin and state of his people and then calls them to "wash yourselves, make yourselves clean; remove the evil of your deeds from My sight" (Isa 1:16). Then Isaiah gives some of the most picturesque illustrations of the change that comes from repentance:

> "Come now, and let us reason together,"
> says the Lord,
> "Though your sins are as scarlet,
> They will be as white as snow;
> Though they are red like crimson,
> They will be like wool." (Isa 1:18)

Later in the opening chapter, God connects his people's redemption with those who repent:

> Zion will be redeemed with justice
> And her repentant ones with righteousness. (Isa 1:27)

As Isaiah turns in the latter chapters to God's promises of restoration, we find several instances where God turns toward or returns to his people. Within our English translations, some of the key terms may not be translated as "turn" or "repent"; however, they are from the trio of Hebrew words that commonly connote repentance. We look closer at these specific words in chapter 4. As I quote verses below, these keywords are underlined.

The first clear instance of God returning to his people is found in Isaiah 40. God says, "'Comfort, O comfort My people,' says your God. . . That her iniquity has been removed'" (Isa 40:1–2). The climax is found in verses 9–11, where the context is God coming to his people:

> Get yourself up on a high mountain,
> O Zion, bearer of good news,
> Lift up your voice mightily,
> O Jerusalem, bearer of good news;

54. Schökel, "Isaiah," 166.

55. Grogan, *Isaiah*, 28.

Lift it up, do not fear.
Say to the cities of Judah,
"Here is your God!"
Behold, the Lord God will come with might,
With His arm ruling for Him
And His recompense before Him.
Like a shepherd He will tend His flock,
In His arm He will gather the lambs
And carry them in His bosom;
He will gently lead the nursing ewes.

The underlined word, while translated as "comfort" in the New American Standard, is used in the Old Testament to connote a change of mind—regret, repent, or console. Again, more is said of this word in chapter 4; however, here and in the verses that follow, we obviously can understand the word is meant to invoke the image of someone, God in this case, turning and coming in response to a change in situation. In this case, that change is the removal of iniquity, the reversal of the fall, and the reforming of a people of God, to the point at which they allow God himself to rule over them.

We find a similar image in Isaiah 52. Again, God addresses Zion, Jerusalem, and says good news is coming, the good news of God's own returning.[56] Within the multitude of returning images, we read, "Break forth, shout joyfully together, you waste places of Jerusalem; for the Lord has comforted His people, He has redeemed Jerusalem" (Isa 52:9). God is returning to his people as King; he will go before them and be their rearguard (Isa 52:12). God's turning to comfort his people comes in connection with his redemption of them; in fact he speaks of them as innocent and oppressed without cause. This chapter also serves as the introduction to the fourth "Servant Song." As we see in detail in the next chapter, God's turning to his people comes literally and physically.

As we have briefly examined these two examples in Isaiah, we are able to see what God is doing. He is dealing with the sin of his people, a people who have turned away from him. Their turning has caused God to turn away, but God will turn back to his people—it is part of his mission. The debate as to who turns first is irrelevant; the biblical witness clearly illustrates a

56. Grogan comments, "This exultant passage contains echoes of 40:1–11. There Jerusalem was given good news about her God, who would come with power and yet gentleness. Here the prophet brings together a number of important themes, virtually identifying peace, salvation, and the kingdom of God, and so reminding us of the NT revelation that Christ's work secures these and every blessing for God's people." Grogan, *Isaiah*, 297.

mutual turning. What is clear is that God calls his people to turn, and if they do, he will be there with comfort, forgiveness, and redemption.

CONCLUSION

We began this chapter by acknowledging a new kind of Christianity has emerged. It is a Christianity focused upon the individual and the individual's desire for God to turn to them and to acquiesce and meet their needs. In this way Christianity has become egocentric rather than missionally focused. It also stands in contrast to what we see in God's mission to call those who have turned away from him to turn back to him.

We have conducted a brief survey through the Old Testament for the purpose of answering our initial question: what is God doing? By examining the creation and the fall (or the turn) narratives, the calling of Abraham and the formation of the covenant, through the promise of the land, and even within the words of the prophets, we have seen part of what God is doing is calling people to turn/return to him. This call to turn/return to God is consistent and clear as we make our way through the Old Testament. Thus, as we seek to understand the *missio Dei* and comprehend the picture God is painting, one dimension of the painting we must see is God's mission to call his people to turn/return as he turns/returns to his people. What we discover in the New Testament is that God turns/returns to his people in the person and work of Jesus.

3

What Jesus Came to Do

As Americans, we relish choice. One stroll down the cereal or potato chip aisle at the grocery store proves the point. Or take the great American staple—the buffet. Instead of choosing one item off a menu, we can fill our plate(s) with everything from salads to vegetables to steak and seafood, and still find room for dessert. While the gluttony represented by the buffet may be an American stereotype, according to Guinness, the record for the largest buffet in the world occurred in Surat-Thani, Thailand, on September 9, 2017. The buffet contained 5,829 different dishes and fed over 30,000 guests.[1]

Whether it's the cereal aisle, the potato chip aisle or the buffet, it all comes down to choice.[2] We get to choose which cereal box or chip bag we pick up. We get to choose which dishes we put on our plate or skip over. We also get to choose to skip the cereal aisle completely and pick up bagels instead. Choice is built into American culture. We see it in our economic system and the competition that is the foundation of capitalism. It is also embedded in our political system. At the heart of democracy is the people's

1. Guinness World Records, "Largest Buffet," paragraphs 1–2.

2. See Hart, *Atheist Delusions*. He writes, "For us, it is choice itself, and not what we choose, that is the first good, and this applies not only to such matters as what we shall purchase or how we shall we live [sic]. In even our gravest political and ethical debates-regarding economic policy, abortion, euthanasia, assisted suicide, censorship, genetic engineering, and so on- 'choice' is a principle not only frequently invoked, by one side or by both, but often seeming to exercise an almost mystical supremacy over all other concerns." *Atheist Delusions*, 22.

ability to choose who governs them. Thus, the egoentric nature of today's evangelical Christianity has its roots in the larger culture of choice as wedded to the concept of individualism.[3]

Choice has come to define the religious climate in America as well. And when we combine choice with religion, we arrive at a place where religions or religious ideas can be taken, left, or mixed in whatever way suits the one choosing. We can walk down the buffet of religious ideas and choose the ones that we want and leave what doesn't satisfy our appetite. Not only that, but, like when a politician runs for office, we want to be courted. Like consumers, we want to be sold to. We want to know how a certain product, or a certain candidate, or even a certain religion can solve the problems we experience.

While that is good and right for politics and makes for good advertising campaigns, there are those in our communities, and some within our churches, who see Jesus walking onto the scene as if he were a candidate running for political office. From this point of view, Jesus recognizes human beings are broken, selfish, and greedy and he proposes one possible solution. Jesus teaches love and tolerance; he does good to others and asks for them to follow his example. Ultimately, he dies because he will not fight back. Today, those who agree with Jesus' proposed way of solving the human dilemma can choose to "vote" for him, while those who do not are equally right to cast their vote for any of the other religions in the world or vote to forgo organized religion entirely. We can choose Jesus off the buffet of options or choose Muhammed, or Buddha, or Caesar. Acceptance or rejection of each is based upon that "candidate's" potential solutions to the issues we face.

If we see Jesus in a similar vein, what then does Jesus come to do? Some see Jesus speaking to issues like marriage, money, humility, generosity, forgiveness, and peace in order to give his opinion on how human beings should live. Once we hear his proposals, if we like his solutions to these issues, as we just saw above, we can vote for his way. If we do not, we can vote for another way. Additionally, accepting one of Jesus' solutions does not necessarily involve accepting all of them. We could vote for Jesus' opinion on forgiveness but reject his opinion on marriage or vice versa. Again, Jesus is just someone proposing one possible solution to the problems of the world; Jesus is one option on the buffet.

For the Christian, however, Jesus should stand as more than a man proposing one of many solutions to the problems found in humanity. The biblical witness, with Jesus' own words as the center-point, affirm Jesus was not one of many ways or one of many teachers who wanted human beings

---

3. See Nanakdewa et al., "Salience of Choice Fuels Independence," paragraph 1.

to simply get along with one another. Neither was Jesus simply giving his opinion on the issues of his day—or our day. He wasn't running a campaign, telling us what we wanted to hear so he would be our choice and win an election. We must choose Jesus, of course, but the reason we choose Jesus matters. Choosing Jesus does not mean merely accepting the teachings we like or the ones that we think meet the needs we have. Rather, choosing Jesus means following. It means joining with Jesus in the reasons why he came. It means joining in Jesus' mission in the world as Jesus is the embodiment of God who came to complete God's mission in the world.

We explored God's mission in the last chapter, but let us recap: God created the world and created human beings to be his people. After the fall, human beings turned away from God and God declared that the fate of every human being was to return to the ground. God, however, would make a way for human beings to return to him. As part of his plan, God called one man, Abraham, and through Abraham God would make a people for himself in a land he would give to the—a new vision of Eden. Through that people, Israel, God would bless the entire world and set the world right.[4] Out of his love for Israel, as his people, God gave them commandments to live by and told them how they were to relate to God and one another. Israel, however, turned away from the one true God and turned to worship other gods. In a repeat of Genesis 3, they were taken out of the land and it seemed as if God's plan was thwarted once again. But God always had a better way: a Messiah. Isaiah especially makes clear, among the passages we mentioned above, God would turn and come to his people. The New Testament writers confirm God did come, literally, in Jesus, his Son.

WHY DID JESUS COME?

The preliminary question, then, is why? Why did God come to his people in the person of Jesus? Jesus came to fulfill the mission of God in the world. Jesus came to launch the transformative plan God had designed long ago and intended all along.[5] God's mission is to make a people who will turn to him, know him, worship him, and be in relationship with him as the one true God. For this to happen, the problem of sin must be dealt with and the reality of God's rule must be proclaimed. Jesus, God with us, comes to fulfill that mission. While this may be old news to some, it is a point that deserves emphasizing because it is the gospel, the good news:

4. See N. T. Wright, *Simply Christian*, where he makes this argument throughout the book.

5. N. T. Wright, *Simply Jesus*, 11.

> What is the mission of this God, about whom the Old Testament affirms such transcendent uniqueness? And in what way is the New Testament confession of Jesus connected not just to the identity and functions of the God of Israel but also to his mission?. . . In the New Testament this divine will to be universally known is now focused on Jesus. It will be through Jesus that God will be known to the nations. And in knowing Jesus, they will know the living God. Jesus, in other words, fulfills the mission of the God of Israel.[6]

These words highlight the very connection we have been making. God desires to be known throughout all of his creation and knowing God means turning to him. However, before we could turn and return to God, God needed to turn to us. God, in Jesus, does just that. Thus, Jesus comes to complete God's mission.[7]

Jesus also comes to invite human beings to experience the mission of God and participate in the mission of God. He does not invite human beings into an egocentric religion where God's mission is to meet every human need and give every human his or her best life. Neither does Jesus come to give his opinion on how human beings might consider living, as if he were trying to win their vote. Rather, Jesus calls human beings to return to a relationship with God, as he incarnates God's mission in the world. He calls human beings, ourselves included, to see God for who he is—the true and only King—and make the change or turn necessary to place ourselves in the right position before him. Jesus' teachings are not just good advice or one way among many; instead, Jesus is showing "people how to live within that whole new world,"[8] that world where God is King, where sin is dealt with and redeemed, and where God's people are back in intimate relationship with him. Our participation in God's mission is explored more fully in a later chapter.

How then did Jesus understand, proclaim, and embody his mission in the world? If we take the gospel accounts for what they claim to be, then we do know how Jesus saw himself fulfilling the mission of God in the world.[9]

---

6. C. J. H. Wright, *Mission of God*, 122–23.

7. See Köstenberger and Alexander, *Salvation to the Ends*, 44.

8. N. T. Wright, *How God Became King*, 47.

9. Mark says his book is the "gospel [good news] of Jesus Christ, the Son of God" (Mark 1:1). Luke describes his work as "an account of the things accomplished among us, just as they were handed down to us by those who from the beginning were eyewitnesses and servants of the word" (Luke 1:1–2). John notes that "these have been written so that you may believe that Jesus is the Christ, the Son of God; and that believing you may have life in His name" (John 20:31).

All Jesus came to do and accomplish encompasses far more than we can attempt to cover here. Our purpose is to note instances where Jesus' mission touches on and furthers the theme of turning and returning within the *missio Dei* explored in the previous chapter. As Jesus engaged in his ministry, he directly addressed this element of his coming on at least four occasions. Jesus said his coming, and thus his mission, was to announce the kingdom of God (Matt 4:17; Mark 1:14–15; Luke 4:43), invite sinners (Luke 5, Luke 15), seek and save the lost (Luke 19), and call a people (Matt 11–12).

As we look at each of these in turn, our purpose is to note how all four of Jesus' statements are either linked by the direct call or come within the context of turning. We must remember Jesus did not come to proclaim his own message, engage in his own mission, or merely give his opinion on the issues facing humanity. Rather, Jesus came doing the will of the Father, preaching the message of God, and thus completing the mission of God. Jesus makes this clear within John's gospel, for example (John 5:19, 5:30–32, 5:36; 7:16; 8:42; 12:49). As we saw, part of God's mission is to have a people who turn to him.[10] And, as we define in more detail in the next chapter, this is a major component of repentance. We must also remember Jesus preached a singular message and came to complete a singular mission: to complete God's promises to Adam, Eve, and Abraham. The promises would be fulfilled and set the world right through the forgiveness of sins, the redemption of God's people, and the declaration that God is King.[11]

Announcing the Kingdom

As Matthew, Mark, and Luke write their accounts of Jesus' life and ministry, they each remember Jesus launching his public ministry by announcing the kingdom of God, also called the "kingdom of heaven." Matthew 4:17 records, "From that time Jesus began to preach and say, 'Repent, for the kingdom of heaven is at hand.'" Similarly, Mark reports, "Now after John had been taken into custody, Jesus came into Galilee, preaching the gospel of God, and saying, 'The time is fulfilled and the kingdom of God is at hand; repent and believe in the gospel'" (Mark 1:14–15). Luke, too, states of Jesus, "But He said to them, 'I must preach the kingdom of God to the other cities also, for I was sent for this purpose'" (Luke 4:43).

---

10. While our focus is on turning within the mission of God incarnated in Jesus, the mission encompasses more than just the redemption of human beings; it includes the redemption of all creation (see Rom 8:19–21; Col 1:20).

11. See N.T. Wright, *Day the Revolution Began*, 346–48; Vanhoozer, *Faith Speaking Understanding*, 85.

As we continue in the gospel accounts, we find Jesus explaining the kingdom of God primarily through parables. Jesus tells stories where the kingdom of God is pictured as a seed sown in a field and with treasure buried in the ground (Matt 13:38, 44). In other places Jesus says the kingdom is like yeast and like a dinner party where the poor, crippled, blind, and lame are invited to attend (Matt 13:33; Luke 14:21–23). As he uses these images, what reality is he describing? When Jesus proclaims the kingdom of God has come, he is announcing that God has come to fulfill what God has promised to do, but it doesn't look like what the people of Jesus' day expected. God would fulfill his promise; not through strength but through sacrifice. Included in this is God coming to form his people into a kingdom and sit over them as their King.

As Americans, the concept of a king and a kingdom may seem foreign. Our perception of kings and kingdoms come from movies or from the few examples of the princes and monarchs remaining in the modern world. Monarchs represent decadence and often tyranny. Frequently, we see their power as corrupt and their rule as absolute. Is the rule of God, incarnated in Jesus, like the rule of the monarchs we see in Jordan, or Saudi Arabia, or even England? No, the kingdom inaugurated by Jesus, with Jesus as King, is a kingdom as described in the parables mentioned above. It is a kingdom of servants and while Jesus, in his resurrection, is given all authority, he rules as the one who emptied himself and became obedient in all things—even to death on a cross (Matt 20:25–28; Acts 1:8; Phil 2:5–11). Thus, the kingdom announced by Jesus and the rule of God as King constitute a reversal of the of the kingdoms we have seen throughout history.[12]

God's kingdom is also not merely a spiritual reality. For Christians it is a lived and experienced reality. Within the continental United States, there are no barriers and many times not even notable signs indicating the movement from one state to another. As one travels from state to state, dialects and idioms may change, local customs may change; however, more importantly, the laws change. The laws of Texas do not apply in Louisiana, and the laws of Louisiana do not apply in Mississippi. Moving from state to state has a real effect on the way life is lived—take how fast one can drive on the highway for example. The same holds true for the kingdom of God. As Jesus comes and announces the kingdom has come in him, "this wasn't just a foretaste of a future reality. This *was* reality itself."[13] And as such men and women who enter into the kingdom and relate to Jesus as King see that the kingdom "works itself out not only in the sanctification of their individual

12. See the Sermon on the Mount, Matt 5:1—7:29.
13. N. T. Wright, *Simply Jesus*, 105.

lives but also in that of every sphere of their common life."[14] The kingdom thus transforms the reality of the world we live in, including the ways we live in common and in relationship with one another.

By using the image of a kingdom, Jesus is tapping into multiple pieces of Israel's history—including prophetic messages and promises made by God.[15] New Testament scholar N. T. Wright emphasizes how Jesus' message of the kingdom fits into the larger story of Israel and God coming to his people: "Israel would at last 'return from exile'; evil would be defeated; [God] would at last 'visit' his people."[16] By using the phrase "kingdom of God," Jesus had a "ready-made slogan" for the mission of God working in and through himself.[17] Another New Testament scholar, Ben Witherington III, highlights Jesus' kingdom message as it relates to Jesus forming a community and a people.[18] The Twelve are chosen, then, as the example of Israel coming back to God as a result of the kingdom's reality.[19] The disciples are a preview of Israel, and later the nations, returning to God as a result of God's kingdom coming on earth.

N. T. Wright also discusses how Jesus redefined the meaning of the kingdom for the people of Israel in his own day. While there is much nuance that goes beyond our purposes here, Wright notes a particular view of the kingdom held by more than merely a "fringe group."[20] Within this view the God of Israel is the only one to rightfully rule, not only over Israel but over the whole world. And if God is the only rightful ruler over the world, it means "Caesar, or Herod, or anyone else of their ilk, is not."[21]

How then would God rule? The answer was an issue of much debate, and the different religious factions in Israel—the Pharisees, Sadducees,

14. Kärkkäinen, *Introduction to Ecclesiology*, 119.

15. N. T. Wright describes five components of Jesus' kingdom announcement: (1) "Jesus' announcement of the kingdom is best seen as evoking the story of Israel and her destiny."(2) A summons to "Israel to follow Jesus in his new way of being the true people of [God]." (3) The story of Israel Jesus told "included a great, climactic ending: judgment would fall upon the impenitent, but those who followed the true path would be vindicated." (4) As the story readjusted symbols from Israel's past, it caused conflict. (5) The immediate conflict was an illustration of "a greater battle, in which [Jesus] faces the real enemy. Victory over this enemy, Jesus claimed, would constitute the coming of the kingdom." N. T. Wright, *Jesus and the Victory*, 200.

16. N. T. Wright, *Jesus and the Victory*, 227.

17. N. T. Wright, *Jesus and the Victory*, 227.

18. Witherington, *Jesus, Paul and the End*, 85.

19. Witherington, *Jesus, Paul and the End*, 86.

20. N. T. Wright, *New Testament and People*, 302.

21. N. T. Wright, *New Testament and People*, 302.

Essenes, Zealots—each had their own vision of what needed to happen.[22] What was consistent, however, was the hope "for the universal divine rule" of God.[23] This became the "liturgy" of Israel "in which the hope was enacted over and over again" through the festivals, Scriptures, songs, and reciting of the history of the nation.[24] When God ruled, there would be a kingdom of God and "Israel's god would become in reality what he was already believed to be. He would be King of the whole world."[25] Thus, as Jesus comes preaching about the kingdom of God, he is not declaring a brand-new message. Rather, he is reorienting the hope of the kingdom upon himself and reconstituting what brings admittance into the kingdom. Instead of the kingdom coming via political or military means, the kingdom comes in Jesus himself and one enters into the kingdom through the act of repentance.

As Jesus preaches the message of the kingdom, he connects its reality to the necessity that one repent. Jesus is not alone in relating the kingdom of God with repentance. John the Baptist preached an identical message: "Repent, for the kingdom of heaven is at hand" (Matt 2:9). The next chapter further defines repentance, but for now we want to see the kingdom constituted a central piece of Jesus' mission and the kingdom is linked to the necessity of repentance. A turning is required because the kingdom has come. The coming of Jesus and the fulfillment of God's mission in him brings with it a new reality. And the response to that new reality is to repent.

The message of the kingdom was previewed by John the Baptist, preached by Jesus, and looked toward the fulfillment of God's mission when God would reign over his people.[26] The response, as well as the expectation, to this act of God, both for John and Jesus, is repentance. Jesus' call to repent is focused, first of all, upon Israel. Jesus' message "addressed not just part of Israel but the whole of Israel, calling her to repentance in view of the in-breaking of the Dominion of God [i.e., the kingdom of God] in and through his ministry."[27] Through repentance, then, Israel would finally

---

22. N. T. Wright, *New Testament and People*, 179–214.

23. N. T. Wright, *New Testament and People*, 303.

24. N. T. Wright, *New Testament and People*, 304.

25. N. T. Wright, *New Testament and People*, 301.

26. Lee references the work of Walter Wink, who notes the parallels between John and Jesus. Lee summarizes by saying, "In short, Wink's analysis shows that unlike the other Gospels, in Matthew, John the Baptist and Jesus are united as allies who inaugurate the kingdom of heaven together." Lee, "Metanoia (Repentance)," 80.

N. T. Wright describes John the Baptist as the "advance guard" for Jesus' own work as both the "chronological and theological starting-point for [Jesus'] own ministry." N. T. Wright, *Jesus and the Victory*, 162.

27. Witherington, *Jesus, Paul and the End*, 131.

see her exile end and be fully and wholly restored.[28] Wright understands Jesus, "in announcing the kingdom, was declaring that Israel's fortunes were being restored. It is therefore highly likely that he would have included the demand for repentance- in this sense [what Israel must do for that restoration to take place] within his proclamation."[29]

After the resurrection, the kingdom expands and comes to include what it was always meant to include, namely the nations. This new community, united under the kingship of God in Jesus, "reaches out to Jews and Gentiles alike with a message of repentance and faith in Jesus the Messiah in the light of the imminence of God's kingdom."[30] The kingdom message is one of transformation, where "the will of God is established to transform all of life . . . it transforms relationship with God, with self, with others, and with the world."[31] Thus, Jesus' kingdom message fulfills key aspects of the mission of God we saw above. Within the announcement of the kingdom of God, we find God is turning to his people and calling his people to turn to him.

Inviting Sinners

Jesus was watching Matthew as he sat in his tax collector's booth and as he walked by, he called for Matthew to leave everything behind and follow him. Matthew did just that and in response to Jesus' call, Matthew threw a party at his home in Jesus' honor and invited his friends—fellow tax collectors, and others whom the religious establishment classified as sinners. When the religious leaders brought the makeup of the party guests to Jesus' attention, he responded, "It is not those who are well who need a physician, but those who are sick. I have not come to call the righteous but sinners to repentance" (Luke 5:31–32). The introductory phrases "I was sent to . . ." and "I came to . . ." constitute the language of vocation.[32] Thus, they help inform us of Jesus' mission and what he came to do.

Jesus is, again, echoing the very mission of God we explored in the previous chapter. God desires for his people to turn from sin and turn toward him. Jesus preaches the same message. In fact, his very purpose in coming is to preach that message, incarnate that message, and thereby proclaim that returning to God is available for even the worst sinner. The Old Testament

28. N. T. Wright, *Jesus and the Victory*, 248.

29. N. T. Wright, *Jesus and the Victory*, 249–50.

30. Köstenberger and Alexander, *Salvation to the Ends*, 67.

31. McKnight, *Community Called Atonement*, 9.

32. N. T. Wright, *Jesus and the Victory*, 651.

prophets testified that when God came to his people, sin would be dealt with. The mission of Jesus, as God incarnate, is to be the means by which God ultimately deals with sin and evil. All of God's purposes, the "coming kingdom of Israel's god," the "real return from exile, the final defeat of evil, and the return of [God] to Zion," would happen and were "coming true in and through [Jesus]."[33]

Since the fall, the question facing all of humanity is: what will God do about sin? How will God reverse its effects and its consequence—which we saw were death and a return to the earth? Throughout the Old Testament we see glimpses into God's plan; namely, God will deal with sin by removing it. Such references are found in Isaiah 1:18; 43:25; and Jeremiah 30, just to cite three. In Jesus, the judgment of God upon sinners becomes God's judgment upon sin. On the cross, God's judgment of sin in the flesh of Jesus Christ brings about the removal and the forgiveness of sins.[34] This forgiveness is offered to all who turn to God. Jesus came to call such sinners to repentance: he calls them to turn to God.

The way God deals with the problem of sin and what actually happens within individuals when sin is dealt with constitute part of the doctrine of the atonement. As noted above, each of these mission statements of Jesus builds on and inform one another; the kingdom message and God's dealing with sin must go hand in hand and "separating them is an act of violence," for in the atonement the kingdom is created.[35] The main point here is to emphasize that Jesus' call for sinners to repent must be seen within the context of his announcement of the kingdom of God and within the *missio Dei*. Scot McKnight says, as God's people, atonement is "not just something done to us, and for us, *it is something we participate in*" as we fulfill Jesus' call to be his witnesses and his ambassadors in the world.[36] As we participate in God's work of atonement, we "join God in the *missio Dei*."[37] If our participation in God's atoning work places us as participants in the *missio Dei*, surely we must see Jesus' own atonement work in light of the *missio Dei* as well. Thus,

33. N. T. Wright, *Jesus and the Victory*, 652.

34. N. T. Wright says, "The punishment has been meted out. But the punishment is on Sin itself, the combined, accumulated, and personified force that has wrecked such havoc in the world and in human lives . . . Paul does not say that God punished Jesus. He declares God punished Sin *in the flesh* of Jesus . . . the apostle could see that what was being punished was Sin itself rather than Jesus himself." N. T. Wright, *Day the Revolution Began*, 287.

35. McKnight, *Community Called Atonement*, 13.

36. McKnight, *Community Called Atonement*, 30–31.

37. McKnight, *Community Called Atonement*, 31.

the way God deals with sin in the atonement is an aspect of the *missio Dei* Jesus comes fulfill.

The repentance of sinners is also the main point of three of Jesus' most famous parables: the Parable of the Lost Sheep, the Parable of the Lost Coin, and the Parable of the Lost (Prodigal) Son (Luke 15). More is said about the Parable of the Lost Son in chapter 7. However, what we can say at this point is the joy felt when the sheep, coin, and son are found is the same joy God experiences when a sinner repents. If, as a parent, you have ever felt the panic when you cannot find your child for even a minute or two, then you also know the joy experienced when your child is found or you lay eyes on him or her again. God experiences the same joy! These stories emphasize repentance is for all sinners and "that no matter who they are, where they are from or what they have done, repentant sinners should be welcomed and joyfully received by others into the community of God's people."[38]

As noted above, one of the definitions of sin in the Old Testament is turning away from God and God's commands. We also saw God's call for his people to turn back to him. Here Jesus resounds and gives illustration to the very same emphasis. Sinners need to experience a turning and a changing from being in one state, a state of sin, to being in a completely different state, a state of wholeness, completion, and forgiveness. This invitation to turn comes from a God who seeks and chases after sinners, and restores them to relationship with him.

In Jesus, sinners are forgiven and sin itself is dealt with. While John's gospel does not explicitly have Jesus using the phrase "kingdom of God," Jesus' preaching certainly remains kingdom focused. John clearly shows Jesus comes for sinners and "offers readers a series of penitential characters."[39] John alone introduces Jesus as "the Lamb of God who takes away the sin of the world" (John 1:29). This is part of the work Jesus comes

38. Nave, *Repentance in Luke–Acts*, 184.

39. Boda and Smith, *Repentance in Christian Theology*, 106. The theme of turning extends to describe the changes that constitute much of John's story: "How, then, does the Fourth Gospel use the motif of "turning" in order to point the way to repentance? Light comes into the world, and shines; we expect certain reactions to this light, and will not be disappointed. Before our eyes the world is divided into those who face the light and follow, and those who turn away. Networks of metaphors spin the story, depicting those who stand, follow, come and see (1:35), who 'believe' (2:23–24) and 'come to the light' (3:20–21), who 'believe and obey' (3:36), who 'hear and believe' and so pass from death to life (5:22–24), who turn from food that perishes to food that endures (6:27), who come and drink (7:37), who are divided one from the other (7:40–44), who are healed and told to sin no more (8:11), who follow and walk in the light (8:12), who hear the shepherd's voice and follow (10:1–4), who have bathed but must continue to wash (13:10), and who must as branches be 'pruned' (15:2)." *Repentance in Christian Theology*, 109–10.

to do; "John describes Jesus' mission in terms of both revelation and redemption."[40] Jesus reveals God and brings redemption, the forgiveness of sins (Col 1:14). As we saw above, Jesus connects his coming for sinners, just like his announcement of the kingdom of God, with repentance. This is the reason Jesus comes to call sinners. As we move toward defining repentance, we now know it is a turning as a response to the arrival of the kingdom and turning or changing to deal with the problem of sin.

Seeking and Saving

The third of Jesus' mission statements to examine is found in Luke 19. When Jesus sees Zaccheus hanging out in the branches of the sycamore tree, Jesus calls to him to come down because he will stay at Zaccheus' house that day. Zaccheus then declares how he will make right those he wronged. In this encounter with Jesus, he acknowledges his sin as he speaks of those he defrauded. We often call this "confession." Additionally, Zaccheus shows repentance through a change of heart resulting in a change in his actions. Zaccheus promises to repay four times the amount to those he defrauded. By affirming salvation, Jesus declares Zaccheus justified and forgiven. As the story closes, Jesus says, "For the Son of Man has come to seek and to save that which was lost" (Luke 19:10).

Jesus' sayings here in Luke 19 coupled with his Parable of the Lost Sheep in Luke 15 echo Jeremiah 50:6[41] and Ezekiel 34:15–16.[42] In both passages God speaks of his people as lost sheep. He comes to seek them out, find them, and restore them. As Jesus resounds these words within his own ministry, he is claiming to fulfill these passages. Jesus comes as the "one shepherd," God's servant, who will gather God's flock so "the Lord will be their God" (Ezek 34:23–24).[43] The message of the prophet Ezekiel is one of hope: "Israel could rejoice; for though she had experienced the cruel and

40. Köstenberger and Alexander, *Salvation to the Ends*, 204.

41. "My people have become lost sheep; their shepherds have led them astray. They have made them turn aside on the mountains; they have gone along from mountain to hill and have forgotten their resting place."

42. "'I will feed My flock and I will lead them to rest,' declares the Lord God. 'I will seek the lost, bring back the scattered, bind up the broken and strengthen the sick; but the fat and strong I will destroy. I will feed them with judgment.'"

43. Alexander comments, "The Lord would deliver Israel from all distress, whether from poor leadership or from the predatory nations. He would do so by appointing one true and responsible Shepherd for his people: the Messiah, his servant David. The Lord would be Israel's God; his servant David, the Messiah, would be Israel's Ruler on earth after he restored Israel to her land." Alexander, *Ezekiel*, 913–14.

incompetent leadership of recent rulers, she now was assured that God would provide perfect leadership through the Good Shepherd, the Messiah, who would care for her as a shepherd should."[44] Once again we see overlapping themes within Jesus' mission: God coming to reign over his people, God dealing with sin, and God seeking his lost people like a shepherd seeking lost sheep.

While the passage in Luke does not contain the words "repent" or "repentance," we can still see the theme clearly within the story. The turn in Zaccheus illustrates repentance. Repentance begins with an acknowledgement of sin and continues through a change of heart and a change of actions. Zaccheus embodies the repentance Jesus calls sinners to in Luke 5. He turns away from sin, as seen in his actions of giving to the poor and paying back those he defrauded, and turns to follow the way of Jesus through a change of heart. We also see justification and forgiveness are the results of repentance.

Calling a People

Matthew 11 contains several sayings of Jesus centered around what he is doing in his earthly ministry and why he is doing it. In Matthew 11, John the Baptist sends messengers to Jesus (John himself is in prison) to ask if Jesus is the "Expected One" or if another is coming (Matt 11:3). John might be wondering why he is still sitting in prison if Jesus is the Messiah. Perhaps in John's eyes, if Jesus is the Messiah, then why hasn't the political revolution begun to take place? In reply, however, Jesus gives several statements about what he is doing. Together they focus on the calling of a people.

First, Jesus gives the reason why he performs signs and miracles. He says in Matthew 11:21 the purpose of his miracles is to bring about repentance. He "denounces" the cities of Chorazin, Bethsaida, and Capernaum because they see his miracles—"the blind receive sight and the lame walk, the lepers are cleansed and the deaf hear, the dead are raised up, and the poor have the gospel preached to them." (Matt 11:5)—but do not repent. The call of Jesus here is not just for individuals to repent but for whole communities to repent.[45] The implication of Jesus' words within the context of Matthew 11 is that because the cities do not repent, they will face divine judgment.

44. Alexander, *Ezekiel*, 914.

45. Lee examines this passage within the view of the universal nature of repentance: "While Matthew 11 and 12 report Israel's refusal of [*metanoia*], they show a universal [*metanoia*], that is the [*metanoia*] of the Gentiles." Lee, "Metánoia (Repentance)," 234. Lee does not, however, note or examine the difference in Jesus calling a community to repentance, not just an individual.

Additionally, within the context of Isaiah 35 (the text Jesus is referencing), these works of God are for the redemption and restoration of his people. By rejecting the works of Jesus, these cities are rejecting the restoration offered as the people of God. Therefore, they will face God's divine judgment.

Second, Jesus declares he does not come to begin a revolution but to offer rest (Matt 11:28–30). Jesus' offer is to all who come to him weary and heavy-laden. The weary who come to Jesus are given rest within their soul, an easy yoke, and a light burden. Here, Jesus seems to be referencing Isaiah 58. Within the Isaiah text, God tells his people to remove the yoke of wickedness and oppression (Isa 58:6, 9). If the yoke of wickedness is removed, God declares, "Then you will call, and the Lord will answer; you will cry, and He will say, 'Here I am'" (Isa 58:9). The turning to God, symbolized by the removal of the yoke of wickedness, precipitates the return of God to his people. Jesus takes this same imagery and expands it. Jesus offers the removal of one yoke and the taking up of another, the yoke of the Messiah. The change described by the removal of one yoke and the taking up of the other mark the people of God.

While a call to repent is only explicitly preached within the context of Jesus denouncing the cities of Chorazin, Bethsaida, and Capernaum, the theme is clearly seen throughout the whole passage. This is especially true when we understand Matthew 11:28–30 in light of Isaiah 58. Jesus is illustrating what his call to repentance means. It is a turning from one yoke to another. It is a change from being under the oppression of wickedness and being weary from a heavy-laden yoke to being under the easy and light yoke of Jesus, the Messiah. The yoke of wickedness leads to judgment, while the yoke of Jesus leads to rest.[46]

Each of Jesus' mission statements describes his purpose and each builds up and further amplifies the others. Jesus comes proclaiming a kingdom where sinners are welcomed in and in which the lost are sought and found and become the people of God. This has been God's mission from the beginning and Jesus comes to complete it. He is not offering one way among many to live morally or simply preaching a new ethic. On the contrary, Jesus comes to fulfill the *missio Dei* and call human beings to turn back to God as his people.

---

46. Here I am reminded of Hebrews 3–4, where God's wrath and God's judgment are the opposite of rest, but rest is a promise of God made to God's people and fulfilled in Jesus.

RETURNING AS A RESPONSE TO JESUS' MISSION

We've seen Jesus has come to complete the *missio Dei* by announcing the kingdom of God, inviting sinners to repentance, seeking and saving the lost, and calling a people. What then is the result of Jesus' message and ministry? How is Jesus asking his listeners to respond, and how is Jesus asking us to respond? Additionally, how do others in the New Testament understand the response to Jesus' message and mission?

One of the clearest answers to these questions is in the words of the apostle Paul in Acts 28:26–28. Paul is in Rome awaiting his potential hearing before Caesar and accepting visitors, including Jews who lived in Rome. Paul presents to them the message of "the kingdom of God and trying to persuade them concerning Jesus, from both the Law of Moses and from the Prophets" (Acts 28:23). When those who refuse to believe begin arguing and leaving, Paul pronounces a word of judgment over them, taken from Isaiah 6:9–10:

> Saying,
> 'Go to the people and say,
> "You will keep on hearing, but will not understand;
> And you will keep on seeing, but will
> Not perceive;
> For the heart of this people has become
> Dull,
> And with their ears they scarcely hear,
> And they have closed their eyes;
> Otherwise they might see with their eyes,
> And hear with their ears,
> And understand with their heart and
> Return,
> And I would heal them."' (Acts 28:26–27)

What is supposed to be the result of hearing, understanding, seeing, and perceiving? The answer is returning; a return to God so healing can come from God. In this passage, Paul is saying the message of the kingdom of God and of Jesus as Lord and Christ—in short, the whole message of the Law and Prophets—is what God has wanted his people to hear, understand, see, and perceive. If and when that happens, the result is God's people will return to him. Paul interprets Jesus' mission and activity in the light of this Isaiah passage and God's mission to turn his people back to himself.

As Paul makes this interpretation of Jesus' mission, he may or may not be referencing the tradition of Jesus, either the oral tradition or, perhaps, an early version of the written sayings of Jesus. Both Matthew and Mark record

Jesus referencing the same passage from Isaiah (Matt 13:14–15; Mark 4:12).[47] The context within the gospels is Jesus explaining why he speaks in parables, but the message is the same: Some will hear, understand, see, perceive, and believe, and those who do will return to God and find forgiveness and healing. But others will not believe; they will reject what God is doing through Jesus. By rejecting Jesus, they are actually rejecting the fulfillment of God's mission in the world. Jesus is also anticipating his own rejection and the rejection of his mission and message.[48] He is saying "the method of [God's] return, and of Israel's release from bondage, would . . . involve a hiddenness and a secret revelation."[49] Yet, those who would have the ears to hear and understand Jesus' message can themselves return to God and find healing.

This is a hugely important point for us to grasp as we seek to understand the relationship between repentance and mission and what it means for the church today. Those who simply want God to meet their needs but want not to have to make significant changes in their lives do not show the kind of response that Jesus requires. Many people today want to rule over their own lives and add Jesus into certain parts of it. Jesus, however, comes with a different message: God has acted in the world, in Jesus himself, to fix the problem of sin and show he alone rules as King over the kingdom. Entering into the kingdom takes what Paul and Jesus himself both declare: hear, understand, see, perceive, believe, and turn. The turning is the result of the hearing, understanding, seeing, perceiving, and believing. And the result of turning is healing, a healing from sin and a returning to the state of humanity in the garden before the turn.

MISSION AND DIVINITY

Before we move on and define repentance in detail, since we have already seen the word referenced in several of the passages above, let's address one more important question: why could Jesus come and fulfill the *missio Dei*? The short answer is: Jesus is God incarnate. Søren Kierkegaard descriptively and succinctly calls Jesus "the God-Man."[50] In explaining this term, Kierkegaard writes, "The God-Man is not the unity of God and mankind . . . The God-Man is the unity of God and an individual man," that man being Jesus.[51] The gospels bear witness to Jesus' divinity in too many places

47. A smaller portion of Isaiah's passage is also quoted in Luke 8:10.

48. N. T. Wright, *Jesus and the Victory*, 236–38.

49. N. T. Wright, *Jesus and the Victory*, 238.

50. Kierkegaard, *Training in Christianity*, 69.

51. Kierkegaard, *Training in Christianity*, 69.

to mention. Jesus' divinity is the highlight in the prologue to John's gospel: "The Word was with God, and the Word was God . . . And the Word became flesh, and dwelt among us" (John 1:1, 14). Later in John's gospel, Jesus is threatened with stoning for making himself, a man, equal with God when he declares that he and the Father are one (John 10:29–33). Jesus' divinity is also the testimony of the early church and the apostles who worshiped Jesus as both Lord and Christ (Acts 2:36).

The longer answer to why Jesus comes is: he is God with us to do what only God could do. This question and these answers are important to our study because Jesus not only comes to fulfill the *missio Dei*; he is the means through which it is fulfilled. It is Jesus who fulfills

> the promise God made to Adam and Eve that Eve's seed will crush the serpent's head (Gen. 3:15). Jesus is what makes good God's promise to Abraham to establish an everlasting covenant to be God to Abraham and his descendants (Gen. 17:6–8). He is the realization of God's word to David to establish from his line a kingdom that would have no end (2 Sam. 7:12–14). Jesus is the vindication of God's self-naming as the one who 'is abounding in steadfast love and faithfulness' (Exod. 34:6; cf. John 1:14) . . . Jesus is the promise-keeping of God made flesh, made good, made gospel.[52]

Jesus also comes as God literally returning to his people to make a way for people to return to God. Jesus' call to repent because God's kingdom has come, his message to repent and believe in the good news of the gospel, and the command to preach repentance in Jesus' name to the nations can only happen if Jesus has God come as a man to fulfill the *missio Dei*. Here we are connecting Jesus' mission to Jesus' identity.

The Old Testament prophets preached messages of turning to God. John the Baptist preached repentance because God's kingdom had come, calling Israel to produce fruit in keeping with repentance, and even performed a baptism of repentance; however, neither the prophets nor John ever preached repentance in their own name. Jesus did (Luke 24:47). In fact, as we'll see in a later chapter, the preaching of repentance in the name of Jesus was central to the mission of the church in Acts. Jesus is able to do what the prophets and John could not; he could center repentance upon himself. Thus, turning to Jesus equates to turning to God. Turning to God through Jesus is possible because Jesus is God; he is Lord and Christ. Who Jesus is as Lord and Christ is the "motivation for changing one's mind and life-direction."[53]

52. Vanhoozer, *Faith Speaking Understanding*, 85–86.

53. C. J. Miller. *Repentance*, 31. He says, "This motivation for changing one's mind

CONCLUSION

This chapter has shown that Jesus comes to fulfill God's mission in the world. This mission includes the call for sinful human beings to turn to God and, through that returning, be formed into the people of God. We have seen how Jesus makes this mission his own. Jesus does not come preaching a different message or to complete another mission. The work of God is consistent and his mission is singular. Within the gospels, Jesus' words and actions are focused on the fulfillment of God's mission. As New Testament scholar Jürgen Moltmann says, "The gospels present the history of Jesus in the light of his messianic mission . . . His mission embraces his proclamation and his acts, his acts and his suffering, his life and his death."[54] That mission is the message of repentance and salvation in the name of Jesus. It is the mission of God to rule as the rightful King of the world, to deal with sin and call sinners, seek and save the lost, and call a people. Each of these involves a turning or change. Each involves repentance—turning from sin to God in obedience to God's rule.

We have also explored the way Jesus incarnates and fulfills the *missio Dei*. As Jesus comes into the world, he comes to complete God's mission, part of which is to make a way for human beings to turn/return to him. As Jesus teaches and explains the reason why he has come, he explains he has come to announce the kingdom, invite sinners, seek and save the lost, and call a people. Uniting these mission statements is a call to repent and turn to God, through Jesus himself. Finally, Jesus is able to fulfill God's mission and center repentance upon himself because he is God with us and is able to do what only God can do.

---

and life-direction is *the lordship of the crucified Savior.*" *Repentance,* 33.

54. Moltmann, *Way of Jesus Christ,* 94.

Part 2

4

Turning to God: What Is It?

Over the last two chapters, we have sought to understand the big story of what God is doing, the *missio Dei*. We have seen a major, yet often neglected, piece of God's mission in the world is to proclaim, "Return to me!" Then we saw how Jesus continues and extends this mission within himself and in what he came to do. So far, we have made references to turning and returning and have used the words "repent" and "repentance" somewhat sparingly. Now we want to turn our attention more explicitly to the words "repent" and "repentance," along with their themes, for the purpose of defining them in their biblical sense.

More than just defining the terms, however, we want to use the terms to more fully understand the essential concept of repentance. We want to answer the question: what is repentance? But we also want to understand how defining the concept helps us understand the whole. To return once more to the analogy of a painting, in the preceding chapters we have looked at the picture as a whole, noting its key features and overall story. However, while we can begin to understand how that painting speaks to our hearts and influences how we see ourselves and interact with the world, we also need to look deeper. We need to talk technique. We need to note the brush-strokes, examine the color palette, and observe the perspective. But as we look closer, as we talk technique, we still do not want to miss the picture. We don't want to miss the entirety of what we have defined as repentance.

The challenge of the present chapter is simple: repentance is difficult to define. Repentance is more complex than the single word implies. In attempting to define repentance, we encounter a problem similar to trying to define good or right. So much of the definition depends upon the context. The same dynamics are present as we attempt to define repentance. However, the hard work of defining it is worth it because our vision of repentance is going to expand and we will be able to see how deep and wide this doctrine actually is.

Since, at this point, we need to get into the nuts and bolts, we have to engage with scholars and theologians who have explored this theme. My intention is to review the vital material in a way that is both thorough and understandable. We'll try to talk shop without getting bogged down in technical language. As we proceed, we would do well to remember some scholarly advice that says it is "important not to lose sight of the connection between biblical *words* and biblical *themes*."[1] The words and the themes of repentance inform one another and, at times, the theme will be present even when the words are not.

LET'S LEARN A LITTLE HEBREW

Just as we began in the Old Testament when we talked about God's mission in the world, our journey of defining repentance will also start in the Old Testament. When we examine the Hebrew words that help define or illustrate repentance, we actually have to mention three distinct words. A couple of these words have already been mentioned above. It is unnecessary for our study to walk through a full biblical theology of repentance within the Old Testament—surveying work accomplished by other theologians.[2] We do, however, want to take a brief look at the Hebrew words that connote repentance and are used within the Old Testament, noting some overarching theological themes, while acknowledging, as Boda notes, repentance in the Old Testament is "multidimensional."[3]

Shub

The Hebrew word used most often to connote the idea of repentance is *shub*.[4] While *shub* is the root for *teshuvah*, which is the word translated "repentance" within the rabbinical tradition and modern Judaism, in the

---

1. Köstenberger and Alexander, *Salvation to the Ends*, 4.
2. See especially Boda, *Return to Me*; Boda and Smith, *Repentance in Christian Theology*.
3. Boda, *Return to Me*, 149.
4. The transliteration of this Hebrew word varies among authors.

Old Testament the literal translation is "turn" or "return."[5] Among its listed definitions are: turn around, repent, return, and turn back.[6] *Shub*, as it is used in the Old Testament, is sometimes used in a literal sense. For example, in Judges 3:19 it means a literal physical turning from one direction to another: "But he himself [Ehud] turned back from the idols which were at Gilgal. . ." In another passage, the word is translated as "return": "They [the spies sent to Jericho, who were let down from the wall of Jericho by Rahab] departed and came to the hill country, and remained there for three days until the pursuers returned" (Josh 2:19).

Metaphorically and theologically, *shub* is used to describe one's position to God—either turning away from or turning toward him. We studied this in some detail in chapter 2; however, let's take a closer look at Deuteronomy 30:1–10. This passage was quoted and referenced in chapter 2; here let's examine the text more closely and note the words and phrases translated from the Hebrew *shub*. The root *shub* is found in verses 1, 2, 3, 8, 9, and 10. The words translated from *shub* are underlined.

> So it shall be when all of these things have come upon you, the blessing and the curse which I have set before you, <u>and you call</u> them to mind in all the nations where the Lord your God has banished you, <u>and you return</u> to the Lord your God and obey Him with all your heart and soul according to all that I command you today, you and your sons, then the Lord your God <u>will restore</u> you from captivity, and have compassion on you, and will gather <u>you again</u> from all the peoples where the Lord your God has scattered you . . . <u>And you shall again</u> obey the Lord, and observe all His commandments which I command you today. Then the Lord your God will prosper you abundantly in all the work of your hand, in the offspring of your body and the offspring of your cattle and in the produce of your ground, for the Lord <u>will again</u> rejoice over you for good, just as He rejoiced over your fathers; if you obey the Lord your God to keep His commandments and His statues which are written in this book of the law, if <u>you turn</u> to the Lord your God with all your heart and soul.

This passage, while long, is worth quoting again for two key reasons. First, it is representative of other Old Testament passages in which *shub* is used to refer to turning or returning to God.[7] While we see several English

---

5. Boda, *Return to Me*, 25; Roberts, *Repentance*, 45.

6. Koehler and Baumgartner, *Hebrew and Aramaic Lexicon*, 1427–29.

7. For other examples see Exod 5:22; 32:31; Deut 4:30; 1 Sam 7:3; Ps 51:13; Joel 2:12, 13; Mal 3:7.

words and phrases used for Hebrew words derived from *shub*, clearly the meaning involves a coming back to or a bringing back or a turning to do over again. Second, this passage helps us see, once again, how this turning, or what we commonly call "repentance," is part of God's desire for humanity. Repentance is part of God's mission in the world to call out a people for himself. From *shub*, we discover repentance is a turning back. We also note *shub* is a turning back not only from sinful actions, but more importantly a turning back to God.

Sûr

Within the Old Testament, the "second most common root [of repentance] is *sûr*," which "is employed for turning aside from or putting aside foreign gods or sinful behavior."[8] At times, *sûr* is translated as "turn aside," but more often it is translated as "remove." Such is the case, for example, in 1 Samuel 7:4, where the context is removing idols: "So the sons of Israel removed the Baals and the Ashtaroth and served the Lord alone." Throughout 1–2 Kings, *sûr* is used in both positive and negative ways to describe either a king who did or who did not remove himself, or turn aside, from following God's commands or a king who either did or did not remove idols and places of idolatrous worship from Israel.[9] The English words translated from *sûr* in the following verses are underlined. In 1 Kings 15:12, we read that Asa "put away the male cult prostitutes from the land and <u>removed</u> all the idols which his fathers had made." Additionally, of Jehoshaphat we find: "He walked in all the way of Asa his father, he <u>did not turn</u> aside from it, doing right in the sight of the Lord. However, the high places were <u>not taken away</u>; the people still sacrificed and burnt incense on the high places" (1 Kgs 22:43). In a negative way we see *sûr* used in 2 Kings 13:2: "He [Jehoahaz] did evil in the sight of the Lord, and followed the sins of Jeroboam the son of Nebat, with which he made Israel sin; he <u>did not turn</u> from them."

As we note these instances of the use of *sûr* within these passages, Terence E. Fretheim observes *shub* is used throughout 1–2 Kings in similar ways. *Shub* is also used to describe the turning from idols and is even used to "evaluate kings negatively or positively."[10] This continuity in definition and connotation between *shub* and *sûr*, as a turning or moving either

8. Boda, *Return to Me*, 26.

9. See 1 Kgs 15:5; 15:12; 15:14; 15:43; 22:43; 2 Kgs 3:2; 3:3; 10:29; 10:31; 12:3; 13:2; 13:6; 13:11; 14:4; 14:24; 15:4; 15:9; 15:18; 15:24; 15:28; 15:35; 17:22; 18:4; 18:6; 22:2; 23:19.

10. Fretheim, "Former Prophets," 40.

toward or away from God, leads us to acknowledge there is a God-ordained way of living from which human beings can deviate and to which they can return. This way of living comes from God and describes the manner in which God desires for his people to live among one another and in relationship with him. Within the passages quoted above, God's standard includes a rejection of idolatry, and a commitment to live a life in accordance with God's covenant relationship. Following the theme of repentance through the Old Testament,[11] we find the call to turn back to God includes other social and economic standards as well. A passage from Carol J. Dempsey describes this:

> From what should Israel repent? All the books of the Latter Prophets mention the transgressions of Israel and Judah. The two kingdoms are guilty of excessive land appropriation (Isa 5:8), the perversion of justice (Isa 5:20), self-centeredness (Isa 58:3a), oppression of laborers (Isa 58:3b), infidelity and disloyalty (Hos 4:1), swearing, lying, murder, stealing, adultery (Hos 4:3), false prophesy (Mic 3:3–5), political and religious depravity and arrogance (Mic 1:7; Ezek 6:4, ect.), apostasy (Jer 2:19), among other transgressions. A people guilty of having broken covenant relationship, they have refused to turn back to God (Jer 5:1; Isa 9:13) despite the prophets' preaching and pleas. The texts of the Latter Prophets identify the root of such transgression, namely, a false, devious, perverse, stubborn, rebellious, and proud heart (see, e.g. Hos 10:2; 13:6; Jer 5:23; 17:9; 49:16; Ezek 28:7; Obad 1:3). Israel has taken its idols into its heart (Ezek 14:4). Thus the people's hearts have not remained one with the heart of their God; they have fallen out of covenant relationship with their God and consequently, right relationship with all other people as well.[12]

Here Dempsey also introduces an idea to which we return in an upcoming chapter: if the root of Israel's sins—and not only Israel's sin but our sin as well—is a "false, devious, perverse, stubborn, rebellious, and proud heart," how then do we even begin a turning? The answer is humility.[13]

---

11. For this, see Boda, *Return to Me*, and Boda and Smith, *Repentance in Christian Theology*.

12. Dempsey, "'Turn Back,'" 49–50.

13. See chapter 7.

Nhm

One more Hebrew word connotes repentance within the Old Testament. *Nhm* stands uniquely among the three Hebrew words in this review because it is the only one "commonly used for divine shifts."[14] The word is used this way in Genesis 6:6–7 to describe God's actions when it states God "was sorry" he made man. Richard Owen Roberts highlights the multiple ways *nhm* has been translated within the King James Version, at times translating the word as "repent" (in a variety of tenses) and as "comfort."[15] Boda notes the "challenge in distinguishing between the meaning of the verbs *šŭb* (*shub*) and *nhm* in the Old Testament."[16] Partly this is because the two verbs appear together, at times with *shub* proceeding *nhm* and at other times with the reverse order.[17] The two words together seem to indicate an action (i.e., turning or returning) along with a change in attitude (i.e., be sorry, relent).[18]

Guy D. Nave Jr. offers a robust examination of repentance within the Greek-speaking world as well as within the Septuagint, the Greek translation of the Old Testament. In the Septuagint, *metanoia* and *metanoeo*, the Greek noun and verb translated as "repentance" and "repent," respectively, are only used to translate the Hebrew *nhm*.[19] "The choice of [*metanoeo*] to translate the root [*nhm*], suggests that the translators wanted to convey the notion of a change in thinking, action or behavior that is motivated by regret, remorse, pity or compassion."[20]

Since the majority of the uses of *nhm* within the Old Testament refer to God, it seems the Hebrew writers and the translators of the Septuagint were making a theological statement as much as a linguistic statement. God does not turn away from his own standard or character; therefore he cannot turn or return from a place he has never departed. Part of God's character, however, is to turn in pity and compassion upon his creation. When we turn toward God, God then turns towards us. Equally true is that when God turns toward us, we are able to turn toward God. Thus, we realize God's righteous anger toward us and our sin is not permanent but can be repented of by God. God is able to turn in compassion toward human beings.

---

14. Boda, *Return to Me*, 26.

15. Roberts, *Repentance*, 44.

16. Boda, *Return to Me*, 26.

17. Boda, *Return to Me*, 27. See Joel 2:14; Jon 3:9; Ps 90:13.

18. Boda, *Return to Me*, 27. Whereas I have summarized Boda by saying a "change in attitude," Boda uses the phrase to mean a change in perspective or behavior.

19. Nave, *Repentance in Luke–Acts*, 111.

20. Nave, *Repentance in Luke–Acts*, 113.

This also means repenting, the ability to turn, to change, to realign, or remove, is a characteristic of God. Paul tells us in Romans 8:29 that God is always in the process of conforming us, as Christians, into the image of Jesus. Hebrews 1:3 tells us Jesus, as the Son, is the radiance of God's glory and "the exact representation of His nature." Thus, being conformed into the image of Jesus also means being conformed into the image of God the Father. As such, we are not called to do or be anything other than what characterizes God, which, as we now know, includes repentance. God does not repent from sin as humans do, but God, as Scripture shows, repents in the way he turns in compassion, love, and action toward us.

REPENTANCE IN THE OLD TESTAMENT

Having studied the Hebrew words that indicate repentance, we would be wise to take up the theme within the different parts of the Old Testament.[21] I am indebted here to the work of several scholars, most notably Mark J. Boda. One of the genuine benefits of Boda's work is his biblical approach to the topic at hand.[22] Both the work he authored and the one he coedited with Gordon T. Smith survey repentance within the various literary genres of the Old Testament. These two works will be our primary guides through the current section.

Torah

The theme of repentance occurs throughout the books and narratives found in the Torah. In certain sections, the Torah illustrates the lack of what we might call "repentance" in the actions of Cain,[23] the Egyptian Pharaoh,[24] or

21. Boda notes other Hebrew verbs "used to express repentance"; however, the three noted in this study represent the vast majority of the words used to describe this theme and are the Hebrew words cited throughout the literature on repentance. Other Hebrew verbs Boda identifies include: "*pnh* ('turn'; Isa. 45:22; Jer. 2:27); *sbb* ('turn back'; 1 Kgs 18:37); *śṭh* ('turn away'; Prov. 4:15); *ḥdl* ('cease'; Isa. 1:16); *rûm* (hiphil; 'stop'; Ezek. 45:9); *ʿzb* ('forsake'; Isa. 55:7; Prov. 9:6); *šlk* (hiphil; 'cast away'; Ezek. 18:31; 20:7); *rḥq* (hiphil; 'remove [sin] far away'; Job 11:14; 22:23); *prq* (Aram. 'break away'; Dan. 4:27 [Hebr. 4:24]); *bdl* (niphal; 'separate oneself'; Ezra 6:21; 10:11; Neh. 10:28) and *zkr* ('remember'; e.g. Ezek 36:31; Ps. 78:35; Eccl. 12:1)." Boda, *Return to Me*, 27–28. Even Boda does no more than list these additional words.

22. See Boda, *Return to Me*, 20–21.

23. See Boda, *Return to Me*, 35.

24. Boda, *Return to Me*, 36–38.

even within the Golden Calf Episode.[25] These instances "in some ways fail to create great expectations for the human side of penitential theology."[26] According to Boda, the Torah emphasizes sin and does not describe or show repentance in any major way. As we already noted in the opening chapter, Boda does not see repentance being a major theme within the Torah, especially within Genesis and Exodus.[27] However, as I argued within chapter 2, the calling of Abraham and God's mission to bless the world through Abraham, as well as the promise of a land and the formation of a people of God, are all a part of repentance. While I disagree when Boda concludes repentance does not play a major theme in the Torah, I agree with him when he says these narratives show repentance begins with God and God is the one who initiates the turning.[28]

Even within these, what we might call "non-acts of repentance," we learn more about what it means. From Cain we learn "the importance of the inner affections to repentance."[29] The incident with Pharoah teaches "repentance may be expressed orally through confession of sin and intention to change, but this must be accompanied by sincerity of heart and a change in behavior."[30] Finally from the Golden Calf we take away that "the only hope for a sinful people is the gracious character of [God]."

Repentance becomes a more important theme through Leviticus–Deuteronomy. We noted an important passage from Deuteronomy above. Through the impartation of the law, as it outlines sin and the way sin is mitigated through offering and sacrifices, the underlying theological proposition is a reality where sin can be recognized, confessed, and atoned for, and our relationship with God restored. These are all pieces of repentance. Additionally, as we noted above, these books also contain several sections of blessings and warnings. Within those sections we noted the focus on God foreknowing his people would disobey and break the covenant, yet God would make a way for their returning. This returning, as we've seen, is part of repentance.

25. See Boda, "Renewal," 5–6.

26. Boda, "Renewal," 7.

27. Boda, "Renewal," 3.

28. Boda, "Renewal," 7.

29. Boda, *Return to Me*, 35–36.

30. Boda, *Return to Me*, 37.

The Prophets

As mentioned above, the Old Testament prophets may be the first who come to mind when we think about God's call to repent and turn to him.[31] The work of the prophets "show that the God of creation, the Lord of history remains faithful to love and to covenant despite the people's infidelities, transgressions, and impenitence."[32] In particular, what the prophets emphasize is "the role that the heart plays in relation to repentance, fidelity, reconciliation, and transformation."[33] Earlier, we saw some of the specific infidelities from which the people of God needed to return. What the prophets make clear is returning to God entails more than sacrifices; it requires a change within the heart. When God's people return to him, he promises to return to them (Zech 1:3; Jer 15:19; Mal 3:7). This return involves a change of heart and is also met, by God, with a change of heart.[34] External changes also must occur, as Jeremiah preaches for example.[35] But outward changes alone do not heal the broken relationship that exists between an individual or a community and God.

Thus, the Old Testament prophets portray repentance as a turning to God. It involves a change in both outward behavior and within the heart. The prophets show repentance is "relational, behavioral, internal, verbal, and sometimes ritual."[36] Additionally, repentance is set within the context of God's promise of a new heart and a new covenant. The prophets also preach repentance is necessary for sins committed and "highlight the inability of humans to embrace the agenda of repentance."[37] This is because repentance does not occur purely by human agency. Rather, God plays the majority role in repentance. This becomes of greater importance as we move into the New Testament.

31. Boda emphasizes that "the Former and Latter Prophets [provide] the most extensive material for the theology of repentance in the Old Testament." Boda, *Return to Me*, 107. In his estimation, "Obadiah, Nahum, Habakkuk, and Zephaniah do not contain material relevant to the theology of repentance." *Return to Me*, 95.

32. Dempsey, "'Turn Back,'" 47.

33. Dempsey, "'Turn Back,'" 47.

34. Dempsey, "'Turn Back,'" 60–61.

35. Boda, *Return to Me*, 92.

36. Boda, *Return to Me*, 107.

37. Boda, *Return to Me*, 107.

Writings

While we clearly associate the Old Testament Prophets with the theme of repentance, we might equally disassociate Psalms and the Wisdom Literature from the theme of repentance. However, even a cursory reading of Psalms reveals many psalms can be classified as penitent.[38] Within this genre Psalm 51, David's song of confession after his act of adultery with Bathsheba, quickly comes to mind.[39] Repentance also emerges as a theme in Job in a unique way.

As Job sits in mourning over the attacks of Satan befalling him, Job's friends admonish him to confess his sin before God. In their perspective, these evils would not happen unless Job is unrighteous because of sin.[40] Through the seemingly endless speeches of Job's friends, Job maintains his innocence and righteousness before God, as he does most forcefully in Job 31. God finally enters the conversation and answers Job beginning in chapter 38. Job responds to God's address by saying, "Therefore I retract, and I repent in dust and ashes."

The word translated here as "repent" comes from the Hebrew root *nhm*. This is one of the few times it is used with a subject other than God.[41] The larger question is, however, if Job did not sin, why did he repent? Boda interprets Job's meaning to be, "Therefore I despise myself, and I change my mind concerning dust and ashes [my morality]."[42] In this interpretation, Job says he has changed his mind about despising his life in view of God and his power, authority, and sovereignty.[43]

Even though Job had not broken one of the Commandments or a specific law, he still had been in a state of misalignment with God because he had seen his life, which is given by God, and over which God sovereignly rules, as something to be despised. Job's response then, once he sees God afresh is to repent, change his mind, change his perspective on his life, and see it in the way God sees it. Thus, in Job we find repentance can also entail

---

38. Richard J. Bautch references Rodney A. Werline's definition of penitent prayer seen within the Psalms: "Penitential prayer is a direct address to God in which an individual, group, or an individual on behalf of a group confesses sins and petitions for forgiveness as an act of repentance." Bautch, "Penitence in the Writings," 68.

39. See Bautch, "Penitence in the Writings," 70; Boda, *Return to Me*, 118.

40. See Boda, *Return to Me*, 110–14.

41. See Boda, *Return to Me*, 112–13. Boda examines the syntax and grammar within this text in more depth than is necessary here.

42. Boda, *Return to Me*, 113.

43. Boda, *Return to Me*, 113.

a change in mind, perspective, or attitude into one that conforms with God's mind, perspective, or attitude.

OLD TESTAMENT CONCLUSIONS

After our survey of repentance in the Old Testament, how then would we define repentance? What does repentance mean? What are its characteristics? In our study so far, several elements have become clear:

1. The translation of the Hebrew words *shub*, *sûr*, and *nḥm* as "repent" or "repentance" is a translation of interpretation, meaning none of them translate literally what we have come to understand as repentance. The literal meaning of the words involves turning, returning, or changing. When used metaphorically and theologically, as in turning to God or turning away from sin, it comes into the theme of repentance, as we have come to understand it.

2. Repentance describes external actions but, more importantly, it also describes a heart change.

3. Repentance is an activity involving human agency but, ultimately, God is the majority agent when it comes to repentance.

4. Repentance includes both turning back to God from sin and turning to God in favor of seeing life, in all its components, in the way God sees them.

As Christians, we gravitate toward the New Testament since it contains the witness of Jesus. In addition, we interpret the Old Testament in light of the New Testament and see the New Testament as the completion and fulfillment of the Old Testament. As we move to define repentance within the New Testament, we must keep our conclusions from the Old Testament in mind, while we seek to understand how the New Testament completes and fulfills the doctrine of repentance.

GEEKING ON GREEK

In his book *Repentance: The First Word of the Gospel*, author Richard Owen Roberts begins by writing, somewhat provocatively, "The first word of the gospel is not 'love.' It is not even 'grace.' The first word of the gospel is 're-pent.' From Matthew through the Revelation, repentance is an urgent and indispensable theme kept at the very forefront of the gospel message."[44] While the authors we are interacting with obviously see the theme of repentance as important within the biblical witness, the question remains how much emphasis the *biblical* writers place on repentance, particularly in the New Testament. We have already seen how turning is central to Jesus' mission, but our task here is to look at the theme of repentance within the whole New Testament in a similar way as in the Old Testament.

Guy D. Nave Jr., while acknowledging repentance plays a central role within the narrative of Luke and Acts, also concludes "the demand for repentance is clearly a far cry from being 'the keynote of the New Testament message.'"[45] Nave is referencing a passage from William Chamberlain's 1943 work, *The Meaning of Repentance*, one of the first modern examinations of repentance written in English:

> This formula, 'Repent ye; for the kingdom of heaven is at hand,' is not only a trumpet blast, but also the keynote of the New Testament message. Not only does it break the stillness of the Judean wilderness, but its reverberations are heard throughout the New Testament, reaching their climax in the thunders of the Apocalypse ... If these words do constitute the keynote, we must understand them before we understand the New Testament.[46]

Nave later concludes, "Outside of Luke-Acts, and with the possible exception of Revelation, the motif of repentance does not have a dominant literary role and presence within the New Testament."[47] In another place, Nave continues in this direction and in his critique of Chamberlain by stating:

> Had the canon founders decided to give primacy to the oldest writings in the New Testament—the letters of Paul—it might have been difficult for Chamberlain to identify repentance as the key to unlock the New Testament. This is not because the concept of repentance is unimportant in Paul's letters, but rather because they contain no specific demand to repent. Outside of the Synoptic Gospels and Acts, an explicit demand to repent is found only in Revelation.[48]

How important, then, is the theme of repentance within the New Testament? While Nave is correct that explicit demands to repent are found

---

44. Roberts, *Repentance*, 23.

45. Nave, *Repentance in Luke–Acts*, 3.

46. Chamberlain, *Meaning of Repentance*, 17.

47. Nave, *Repentance in Luke–Acts*, 135–36.

48. Nave, "'Repent, for the Kingdom,'" 87–8.

only within the gospels and Revelation, does that mean Chamberlain is wrong to see repentance as the "keynote" of the New Testament? Who, Nave or Chamberlain, views the importance of repentance in the New Testament correctly? I concede "keynote" may be too strong a description. One could easily argue the keynote of the New Testament is messiahship, lordship, salvation, or grace. However, if we think not of a singular keynote but of a melody heard throughout the New Testament from the gospels, to Acts, to the epistles and Revelation, then repentance is definitely a note helping to tie the melody together. As we have seen, the theme remains essential within the New Testament as much as it is fundamental within the Old Testament. Therefore, Nave, who does see repentance as a major theme of Luke–Acts, does not stand entirely correct. Repentance, as examined below, does indeed permeate the New Testament in its theology and helps constitute the mission of Paul and the early church. In fact, even Nave seems to want to have it both ways. Immediately after declaring that repentance is not a "dominant literary role and presence within the New Testament," he states:

> Nevertheless, the few explicit references to repentance present in the New Testament do suggest that repentance has a foundational role within early Christianity. With the use of summary statements, Mark stresses the fact that repentance comprised the content of the preaching of John the Baptist, Jesus, and the apostles. The message of repentance was at the center of early Christian preaching. Furthermore, Hebrews identifies repentance as part of the foundational teachings of early Christianity.[49]

Verb and Noun

Before we engage in a brief overview of repentance within the New Testament, it is wise for us to understand what specific words we are talking about when we reference repentance in the New Testament. The Greek words translated as "repent" and "repentance" are *metanoeo* and *metanoia*, respectively. Combined, they are used fifty-six times within the New Testament.[50] We find the words used in Matthew, Mark, Luke, Acts, Romans, 2 Corinthians, 2 Timothy, Hebrews, 2 Peter, and Revelation. The challenge

---

49. Nave, *Repentance in Luke–Acts*, 136.

50. The full list of usages is as follows: Matt 3:2, 3:8, 3:11, 4:17, 11:20, 11:21, 12:41; Mark 1:4, 1:15, 6:12; Luke 3:3, 3:8, 5:32, 10:13, 11:32, 13:3, 13:5, 15:7, 15:10, 16:30, 17:3, 17:4, 24:47; Acts 2:38, 3:19, 5:31, 8:22, 11:18, 13:24, 17:30, 19:4, 20:21, 26:20; Rom 2:4–5; 2 Cor 7:9, 7:10, 12:21; 2 Tim 2:25; Heb 6:1, 6:6, 12:17; 2 Pet 3:9; Rev 2:5, 2:16, 2:21, 2:22, 3:3, 3:19, 9:20, 9:21, 16:9, 16:11.

comes as we attempt to discover what each biblical author and the biblical audience understood the meaning of the words to be as they used them within their context.

While *metanoeo* and *metanoia* are the two Greek words most commonly associated with repentance, two other Greek words must be noted briefly as well: *epistrephó* and *metamelomai*.[51] *Epistrephó* means to turn or return and is used in a similar way to the Hebrew *shub*. At times it is used to describe a physical or literal turning or returning, as in Matthew 12:44. However, it also is used to describe a turning or returning to God. Such a use is found in Luke 1:17 describing John the Baptist: "It is he who will go as a forerunner before Him in the spirit and power of Elijah, to turn the hearts of the fathers back to the children, and the disobedient to the attitude of the righteous, so as to make ready a people prepared for the Lord." Within the quotation from Malachi 4:6, the Hebrew word for turn, *shub*, is translated into Greek by *epistrephó*.

The Greek word *metamelomai* is translated in the New Testament as "regret," "remorse,"[52] or even "repent"—which is the common translation within the King James Version. *Epistrephó* is found thirty-six times in the New Testament, while *metamelomai* is used only six times. Within the thirty-six uses of *epistrephó*, twenty-one times it is used to describe turning to God or is used in connection to repenting (i.e., repent and turn). While *metamelomai* is translated most frequently as "repent" in the King James Bible, its usages in the New Testament speak of regret or remorse at a certain action. At times this regret leads to a change of behavior; however, at other times it does not. Together these Greek words compose the theme of repentance within the New Testament. While some references are made to *epistephó* and *metamelomai*, the main focus of this discussion is on *metanoeo* and *metanoia*.[53]

Without diving into a full examination of the uses of *metanoeo* and *metanoia*, we shall proceed directly to some conclusions. After reviewing the terms in a number of works within the Greek world outside of the New Testament, Nave concludes the words "were used to denote an intellectual

---

51. See Boda, *Return to Me*, 163–64; Bailey, "Repentance in Luke–Acts," 53–58; Humphrey, "'And I Shall Heal Them,'" 109–10; Porter, "Repentance in the Epistles," 128–29.

52. Boda, *Return to Me*, 164.

53. Examination of the uses of *metanoeo* and *metanoia* within the Septuagint, Pseudepigrapha, Apocrypha, Dead Sea Scrolls, Philo, Josephus, Plutarch, and other Greek literature is available in the work of other scholars. See Nave, *Repentance in Luke–Acts*; Kintu, "Repentance in the Sermon"; Bailey, "Repentance in Luke-Acts."

change of mind as well as an emotional sense of regret or remorse."[54] Offering a similar conclusion, Bailey notes, "There are numerous texts in Hellenistic literature which use [*metanoeo*] and [*metanoia*] to express various changes in the mind, will, emotions, and even behavior."[55] After such a survey, the question then becomes: did the biblical authors use *metanoia* and *metanoeo* in the same way as these Greek authors or did they use the words in new ways or redefine them altogether?[56]

REPENTANCE IN THE NEW TESTAMENT

As I have reviewed others' works and the New Testament texts, I note six key observations and conclusions that can be made. While these observations and conclusions are supported by the biblical texts and by the work of the scholars who have taken a biblical theology approach to these passages, I have not seen another work summarize the observations and conclusions in the same way I have here. As we seek to define repentance in the New Testament, there are six pieces central to helping us understand the vast meaning of repentance.

1. Repentance Is a Response to God

The first observation we can make from reviewing the biblical texts is that repentance is a response to what God has done. We saw from the Old Testament that God is the majority agent when it comes to repentance. This is amplified in the New Testament. John the Baptist and Jesus preach a message of repentance that is both in response to and made possible because the kingdom of God has come (Matt 3:2, 4:7; Mark 1:4, 1:14–15, Luke 3:3).

When Jesus explains the meaning of the kingdom, one common feature is that the way of the kingdom of God (i.e., the way of God himself) is the way that appears counterintuitive, at least initially. The kingdom is like a mustard seed, a little bit of yeast, a net that traps all kinds of fish, or the

54. Nave, *Repentance in Luke–Acts*, 59. Also see Nave, *Repentance in Luke–Acts*, 39–70.

55. Bailey, "Repentance in Luke–Acts," 106.

56. Bailey proposes a complete redefinition, especially within Luke's usage of the words, saying, "Although Luke presents repentance in a manner that was appropriate for his Hellenistic audience, he is still writing as a Christian, to Christians, about a Christian practice . . . Luke's understanding of repentance is unique in its religio-historical context and significant in its contribution to his theology. His view of repentance is unique in combining Jewish, Christian, and Greek ideas in a manner which has no clear precedent." Bailey, "Repentance in Luke–Acts," 4–5.

promotion of the last and the demotion of the first. These images illustrate the different perspective through which God views life. Repentance, therefore, is a "change of thinking that usually leads to a change of behavior and or way of life."[57] More than that, however, it is what we saw in Job, a changing of perspective that begins to see the world in the way God sees it. As Jesus inaugurates the kingdom of God and declares it has come in himself and in his life and ministry, Jesus stands as the majority agent—God returning to his people—who makes repentance both necessary and possible.

Of course, this is highlighted further in the command to preach repentance in Jesus' name (Luke 24:47). In the same way salvation is found in the name of Jesus and baptism is performed in the name of Jesus, repentance is also preached and performed in the name of Jesus. Notably the command to preach repentance in the name of Jesus comes after the crucifixion and resurrection. It is a response to God's act of love shown in the death and rising of Jesus. Had Jesus not been obedient to the Father to go to the cross, repentance could not be proclaimed in the name of Jesus. As we saw in the previous chapter, Jesus centers repentance upon himself. Any and all repentance occurs as a response to what God has done.

2. Repentance Brings Evidence

Secondly, through a review of repentance in the New Testament we find repentance brings evidence. John the Baptist introduces this concept in Luke 3:8 by calling his hearers to "bear fruit in keeping with repentance." Elsewhere the evidence of repentance comes from deeds to be performed by those who do repent. We find this in Paul's words in Acts 26:20 and in Jesus' message to the church in Ephesus in Revelation 2:5. The deeds or fruit of repentance are deeds consistent with the kingdom and what men and women should do when Jesus is King. John the Baptist gives a series of examples of what the fruit of repentance looks like. John preaches that repentance brings generosity with the poor and integrity and justice in dealing with others (Luke 3:10–14). These deeds are "not simply a matter of the prosperous and powerful learning to share with the poor; it is a matter of all people learning to share with and treat others fairly, justly, and equitably."[58]

57. Nave, *Repentance in Luke–Acts*, 145.

58. Nave, *Repentance in Luke–Acts*, 153. Nave comments elsewhere: "Because of the Lukan addition of the ethical preaching of John the Baptist, at this point in the narrative the reader understands repentance to be associated with bearing fruits of ethical social behavior. The reader understands repentance to address the manner in which human beings interact with each other. It entails the rejection and abandonment of one's former ways of thinking and living and the adoption of new ways of thinking

Matthew also records John the Baptist preaching on the fruit that comes with repentance. The image of fruit occurs throughout Matthew's gospel and represents an "emphasis on righteousness, [and] doing the will of God."[59] The use of fruit then illustrates "the changing (or turning) of one's mind, heart, will, and conduct, thus one's whole being and life."[60] Additionally, it is "doing good, righteousness, and the will of the Father [that] comprise the fruits worthy of [*metanoia*]."[61]

Paul also preaches the "deeds appropriate to repentance" (Acts 26:20). We look more at repentance within Paul's mission in chapter 5. What we want to note here is that Paul understands repentance brings about certain appropriate deeds. Within the context of Acts 26, Paul seems to be referring to the turning "from darkness to light and from the dominion of Satan to God" (26:18). Then within Paul's letters he is more specific in the deeds of repentance and reminding believers what turning from darkness to light and from the dominion of Satan to God entails.

Jesus himself calls the church in Ephesus to repentance with evidence in Revelation 2:5: "Therefore remember from where you have fallen, and repent and do the deeds you did at first; or else I am coming to you and will remove your lampstand out of its place—unless you repent." While Jesus commends some of their works, he chastises them for leaving their first love (2:4). Turning to love Jesus is a deed of repentance.

As we look at repentance as a whole, we also see evidence of repentance is an entirely changed life. Throughout the gospels, Jesus calls on men and women to follow him; however, "responding to the call of Jesus is not about following Jesus while trying to maintain one's present way of thinking and living. Responding to the call of Jesus includes following Jesus, but it also includes forsaking everything."[62] The forsaking required by Jesus includes turning and forsaking one's life of previous sin and turning toward God. The evidence of such turning is a new way of living in light of the kingdom of God; "therefore, the inauguration of the reign of God requires individuals

---

and living that result in the just, merciful and equitable treatment of all people by all people. Therefore, since Jesus defines what he is calling sinners to as repentance, the reader expects this type of abandonment of one's former ways of thinking and living and the adoption of new ways of thinking and living to be what Jesus is calling sinners to." *Repentance in Luke*–*Acts*, 166.

59. Lee, "Metánoia (Repentance)," 89.

60. Lee, "Metánoia (Repentance)," 89–90.

61. Lee, "Metánoia (Repentance)," 90.

62. Nave, *Repentance in Luke*–*Acts*, 168.

to change the way they think about sin and the way they live: it demands a reorientation of life."[63]

3. Repentance Is for Everyone

The New Testament writers clearly proclaim everyone needs to repent, and repentance is for everyone.[64] The calls of John the Baptist and Jesus to repent because the kingdom of God has arrived were universal calls. John the Baptist explicitly called for repentance from the Pharisees and Sadducees in Matthew 3:7–8. These two groups represent those we find even today who believe they are too saintly for repentance. We may think just because we can't point to a specific sin, we are not in need of repentance. However, as we saw with Job and see in the Pharisees and Sadducees, even an attitude misaligned with God requires repentance. Repentance of the Pharisees and Sadducees stands in addition to repentance by tax collectors and soldiers (Luke 3:12, 14). Jesus continues this theme in his own preaching and ministry. Michael J. Ovey understands Jesus' universal call to repentance as one of Luke's major themes.[65] As Luke progresses within his gospel, "the class of 'sinner' is gradually extended to cover even the apparently law-keeping Pharisees. The implication is if even the Pharisees must be classed as sinners, then surely all must be."[66] Thus, Jesus' call, like the call of John the Baptist, includes everyone.

This is echoed, of course, in Acts. On Pentecost Peter calls on each one listening to his message to repent and be baptized in the name of Jesus Christ (Acts 2:28). Peter preaches the same message in Acts 3. Paul also reports on his way to Jerusalem that he had completed his mission and did not "shrink" from testifying that both Jews and Gentiles need to repent (Acts 20:20–21). Paul repeats this same claim a few chapters later in Acts 26.

Another key text is found in 2 Peter 3:9, where Peter writes, "The Lord is not slow about His promise, as some count slowness, but is patient toward you, not wishing for any to perish but for all to come to repentance." One scholar notes repentance in this verse is mentioned "almost inadvertently" and "does not develop the notion in any significant way."[67] However, at this point in his letter Peter is explaining God's coming judgment and when that judgment will take place. Part of Peter's commentary is to remind these

63. Nave, *Repentance in Luke–Acts*, 133.

64. Watson, *Doctrine of Repentance*, 32, also makes this observation.

65. Ovey, *Feasts of Repentance*, 8

66. Ovey, *Feasts of Repentance*, 35.

67. Porter, "Repentance in the Epistles," 144.

Christians that God is judge but God is first wanting all people to repent because repentance moves someone from being under God's judgment to being alive.

Repentance is for Pharisees, Sadducees, Jews, and Gentiles; churches and communities are also called to repent. We have already noted Jesus' words to the cities of Chorazin and Bethsaida and his call for those communities to repent (Matt 11:21). We also saw Jesus calling the church in Ephesus to repent. As Jesus speaks to the churches of Asia Minor in Revelation 2–3, he also calls the church of Pergamum and the church of Sardis to repent. Within Revelation, repentance applies to "both the Christian community and the world."[68]

What does it mean then for a church to repent? In many ways, it is not all that different from repentance as an individual. A church, just like a person, can turn away from God. A church can stop obeying God or even turn away to worship the idols of attendance, power, money, or emotion. A church in such position is therefore called to repent. It is called to turn, return, and change and realign itself with God.

4. Repentance Is for Sins

The New Testament, in uniformity with what we saw in the Old Testament, declares repentance is needed in response to sins committed. John the Baptist preaches this message in Mark 1:4: "John the Baptist appeared in the wilderness preaching a baptism of repentance for the forgiveness of sins." Jesus also preaches repentance as a response to sin, as we saw in Luke 5:32. The repentance of sinners constitutes a major theme in Luke and is seen throughout the book. This theme continues in Luke 15, where God rejoices "more over one sinner who repents than over ninety-nine righteous persons who need no repentance" (Luke 15:7). The parables in Luke 15 "clearly [convey] that repentance should be responded to with joy and celebration because repentance delivers sinners who were once lost and perishing."[69] Continuing in Luke, we find a similar link between repentance and sin in 17:3–4 and 24:47.

Repentance as a response to sins is also a consistent theme in Acts, as we would expect, since Luke authored both volumes. Peter, as he preaches in Acts, calls on his audience to repent and be baptized "in the name of Jesus Christ for the forgiveness of your sins" (Acts 2:38), to "repent and return, so that your sins may be wiped away" (3:19), and that Jesus was exalted

68. Humphrey, "'And I Shall Heal Them,'" 117.

69. Nave, *Repentance in Luke-Acts*, 183.

in his death and resurrection to "grant repentance to Israel" and forgive sins (5:31). This theme continues throughout Acts, the letters of Paul, and Revelation.

Repenting for sins is probably the most well-known aspect of repentance. Within the Westminster Confession of Faith, repenting for sins is part of what is called "Of Repentance unto Life." Article 2 reads:

> By it [repentance], a sinner, out of the sight and sense not only of the danger, but also of the filthiness and odiousness of his sins, as contrary to the holy nature and righteous law of God; and upon this apprehension of His mercy in Christ to such as are penitent, so grieves for, and hates his sins, as to turn from them all unto God, purposing and endeavoring to walk with Him in all the ways of His commandments.[70]

The words of the Confession help us see the turn repentance brings as a turning from the ugliness of sin and a turning back to following the ways of God. This turning perhaps most clearly takes place at conversion. That being said, repentance and conversion, while they are related, are not synonymous.[71] Rather, there are three main problems in seeing repentance and conversion as synonymous. Taken individually, these three problems may be accounted for, but taken together, they render implausible equating repentance and conversion.

First, making repentance and conversion synonymous would make New Testament repentance completely different from Old Testament repentance. As we have seen, the Old Testament presents repentance as a turning or returning of primarily God's people to God. There is no emphasis on one *converting* from one thing to another.

Second, seeing repentance and conversion as synonymous would make repentance in the New Testament completely different from its use in the non-biblical Greek literature we saw above. There, the meaning of repentance is a changing of mind or a changing of behavior. Again, there is no indication of a conversion from something to something else.

Third, understanding these words as synonymous simply doesn't make sense within the context of the New Testament. For example, the joy in finding the lost sheep or lost coin, or the joy in the returning of the lost son, is not because they have converted but because they are found. Additionally, it would make no sense within the usages of "repent" in Acts.

---

70. Roberts, *Repentance*, 65.

71. Several theologians have proposed repentance and conversion describe essentially the same thing. Reviews of these positions are found in Bailey, "Repentance in Luke-Acts."

When Peter in Acts 3:19 calls on his hearers to "repent and return," he is echoing the language of the Old Testament prophets; the prophets do not call for conversion. Additionally, throughout Acts repentance is preached to both Jews and Gentiles. If repentance is synonymous with conversion, what are Peter and Paul calling Jews to convert to? Peter, Paul, and others are not "converting" Jews or Gentiles to "Christianity," but rather calling them to turn to God, or return to God (repent), through the work of Jesus, the Messiah. One of the clearest examples of this is in Acts 26:19–21. There Paul asserts he has declared everywhere, to both Jews and Gentiles, a message of repentance—which he defines as turning to God. Thus, if repentance merely equates to conversion, it would redefine the concept for Jews as well as Greeks, and change the understanding of the uses of "repent" throughout the New Testament.[72] While repentance is a *part* of conversion, to equate the two as synonymous is not credible.

5. Repentance Saves from Divine Consequences

As we follow the theme of repentance through the New Testament, we find several instances where Jesus pronounces warnings to those who are unrepentant. We find these words in Matthew 11:20–21 (Luke 10:13–15), in a passage we have examined in another context above. Another direct statement from Jesus is found in Luke 13:1–5, where twice Jesus says, "I tell you, no, but unless you repent, you will (all) likewise perish" (13:3, 5). These warnings build upon the warnings of John the Baptist in Matthew 3:10 and its parallel in Luke 3:9.[73]

What are we to make of these warnings by John the Baptist and Jesus seen in the gospel accounts? They both teach that failure to repent brings consequences. Certainly, this includes natural consequences, whether socially, relationally, economically, physically, or judicially, but there are also ultimate divine consequences as all sin is, ultimately, against God. John the

72. I disagree on this point with the work of Nave in *The Role and Function of Repentance in Luke–Acts*. Nave understands repentance for Jews and Gentiles as being different (*Repentance in Luke–Acts*, 213). For Nave, repentance for Gentiles merely involves that they believe in Jesus on the one hand, but also that they change their thinking about their "idolatrous and pagan practices," on the other hand (*Repentance in Luke–Acts*, 213–14). He too makes repentance and conversion synonymous, at least when Gentiles are involved. However, as I explain above, Paul does not make a distinction between the message of repentance he declares to Jews and the message of repentance he declares to Gentiles. For Paul, they are the same message and not a message that we find merely synonymous with conversion.

73. Matt 3:10: "The axe is already laid at the root of the trees; therefore every tree that does not bear good fruit is cut down and thrown into the fire."

Baptist understands the consequences as like a fire that consumes the chaff (Matt 3:12). The repentant, those who repent in light of the coming of the kingdom of God and produce fruits worthy of repentance, are gathered like wheat, whereas the unrepentant, the chaff, are burned up with "unquench-able fire." In Luke 13, Jesus uses two contemporary illustrations (the Galile-ans Pilate had killed, and the tower that fell in Siloam and killed eighteen) to show the way to life, as opposed to perishing, is not because some are better than others (i.e., they commit fewer sins, or commit sins deemed less significant than other sins) but because one has repented.[74]

While this same theme can be seen in other New Testament passages, one of the major texts comes from the apostle Paul in Romans 2:4–5. This passage both highlights God's grace in wanting everyone to come to repen-tance, and warns that the consequence of not repenting is the wrath of God that will come on the day of God's judgment. The failure of repentance is not due to God, but rather to "the stubbornness" of human beings.[75] Such unre-pentant persons, Paul declares, "are accumulating for themselves the wrath of God, which will come in a dreadful day when God's righteous judgment is revealed—even though it is being withheld to this point."[76]

6. Repentance Occurs in the Context of Relationship

Throughout the instances where we see repentance in the New Testament, we cannot help but understand them within the context of relationship. Repentance brings us into the community of the kingdom of God (Matt 4:7; Mark 1:14–15). Repentance restores the relationship between the one lost, humans, and one seeking the lost, God himself (Luke 15). Thus, the

---

74. Nave comments on this passage, saying, in part, "the Lukan Jesus makes it clear that only repentance can deliver sinners from perishing." Nave, *Repentance in Luke-Acts*, 179. Nave also sees a relationship between Luke 13 and Luke 15. In Luke 13, "those who fail to repent are the ones who end up perishing; throughout Luke 15, however, repentance serves as a corrective for [perishing]." *Repentance in Luke-Acts*, 179. The word translated perish in Luke 13 and the word translated lost in Luke 15, are the same word. *Repentance in Luke-Acts*, 179. Thus, to be lost and separated from God is to perish and to perish is to be lost. I do, however, disagree with Nave's interpretation of this passage. He understands Jesus to be saying that those Pilate killed and those killed by the tower were killed because they did not repent, not because they were sinners. *Repentance in Luke-Acts*, 178. Jesus' point, as I interpret the passage, is based upon the biblical fact that everyone is a sinner, but those who were killed were not greater sinners than anyone else. Everyone, therefore, is under the warning of coming perishing, unless one repents.

75. Porter, "Repentance in the Epistles," 131.

76. Porter, "Repentance in the Epistles," 132.

renewal of the relationship between humans and God includes repentance. Repentance also restores relationships between individuals as we turn away from the sin we commit against one another and practice forgiveness (Luke 17:3–4). Additionally, repentance is central in forming the community of the church as seen in Acts. On this point, Chamberlain correctly says, "Repentance is a pilgrimage from the mind of the flesh to the mind of Christ. The mind of Christ is necessary to full fellowship with Christ."[77]

Unsurprisingly, others who have studied repentance have noted repentance occurs within the context of relationship. What is surprising is it doesn't seem to be a point of emphasis. Nave comments on the relational aspect of repentance in fleeting remarks in several places. In one place he writes, "Repentance may represent an individual decision, but it often transforms social relationships."[78] Nave is specifically speaking of "correcting economic and social disparity among people" as seen in the preaching of John the Baptist.[79] Certainly, a turn from sin, seen in the exploitation of others through abuse, neglect, or indifference, will bring a correcting of some economic and social disparity, but the context of relationship extends beyond merely that. Other instances where this lack of emphasis on repentance and relationship, especially in connection with the church, were noted in the introduction of the current work, including Walter Brueggemann and Michael J. Ovey, each of whom notes that exploring the fullness of repentance in the context of relationship is important; Brueggemann calls it the "next question" needing to be answered.[80]

This is unquestionably true, and one of the reasons for this present work. The task of connecting repentance and the mission of the church involves, as Ovey says, "the corporate life of the people of God."[81] God's mission, as we have seen, is to have a people who turn to him in a loving relationship as the one creator God. Jesus came to incarnate this mission, and the church is sent into the world to proclaim this mission. The relationship context of repentance is central and is an undercurrent we see throughout, especially when we focus on the church, as the church is, in part, a community of people in a relationship with God. As we move toward the conclusion of this chapter, Stanley E. Porter summarizes these six observations and conclusions well, saying:

77. Chamberlain, *Meaning of Repentance*, 47.

78. Nave, *Repentance in Luke–Acts*, 158.

79. Nave, *Repentance in Luke–Acts*, 159.

80. Brueggemann, "Summons," 349–50.

81. Ovey, *Feasts of Repentance*, 6.

Repentance is not the first step in remedying the relationship between God and humanity since that first step is taken by God, who is the author and provider of forbearance, patience, and kindness; however, it is the human response in terms of behavior. God's gracious and evident provision is what should motivate the sinful human to repentance, that is, to turn from hard-heartedness deserving of God's righteous anger.[82]

A DEFINITIVE DEFINITION?

After all this work, then, are we now able to give a definitive definition of repentance as we see and understand it in the Bible? The answer is, surprisingly, no. Every author who writes on repentance proposes one or sometimes several definitions of repentance. Many of these definitions share similar words and themes, but it seems impossible to create *the definitive* definition of repentance. This chapter has shown why a definitive definition is so hard to formulate. The Hebrew and Greek words we translate as "repent" and "repentance" or carry the idea of repentance, even if the word is not used, carry with them the weight of an idea. In Hebrew it's a metaphorical idea taken from a literal turning or returning. In Greek the idea connotes several ideas ranging from its non-biblical uses to its biblical uses—which have been the focus of the current review.

Because a definitive definition remains elusive, the purpose of our exploration in this chapter has been to examine repentance much like a work of art. To return to our opening analogy, we have talked about the technique that formed the painting of repentance. A great painting cannot be defined, but its features can be explored and its meaning discovered by looking at the parts of the painting in their relationship to the whole. In a similar way, a great symphony does not render itself to a definition; rather we can examine pieces, movements, and instruments in relation to the whole work. This examination has done the same thing.

Repentance has been examined in its parts but, more importantly, within the relation of the parts to the whole. We have talked about technique, not to become a master at technique, but to become more aware of the whole picture. What then are we able to say about repentance and its meaning within the Bible? A better question, perhaps, is: what is the picture repentance that paints as we look at it in its entirety? That is the question this chapter has sought to answer. The picture we gain of repentance is a picture of turning back to, returning to, coming again, turning away from

82. Porter, "Repentance in the Epistles," 132.

one thing to another, which occurs in the heart and in a response to God's agency. It is a picture of realigning with God. It is a picture centered on God, as God is the one to whom all the action points. It is a response to God; it brings forth evidence when it occurs; it is for everyone; it is for sins; it saves from divine consequences; and it occurs in the context of relationship.

CONCLUSION: SEEING THE PICTURE

When we see the picture in its entirety, it is a beautiful picture indeed, because in it we see the mission of God. What we explored in the Old Testament as God's mission to have his people turn/return to him and what we saw incarnated in Jesus' ministry in the New Testament as he fulfilled God's mission in the world is a mission of repentance. As the words "repent" and "repentance" were used through the opening chapters, their use was preparing for this larger study. Now we see repentance does, in fact, describe God's mission in the world. From the Old Testament, to Jesus, to today, God is on a mission of repentance. God turned to humanity in the incarnate work of Jesus in order that humanity could turn to him. After this chapter, we see what turning to God entails and we see it constitutes a major part of God's mission in the world. Now let's turn and begin to look at what repentance means for the mission of the church today.

5

The Church and the Mission of Repentance

IN 2020, A *BuzzFeed News* article was published outlining a culture of harassment prevalent within the production of *The Ellen DeGeneres Show*. In all, thirty-six former employees described a toxic work culture that included instances of racism, sexual assault, and a general "demeaning" attitude toward employees.[1] In response to the allegations, DeGeneres offered an apology, saying in part, "As you may have heard, this summer there were allegations of a toxic work environment at our show and then there was an investigation. I learned that things happened here that never should have happened . . . I take that very seriously and I want to say I am so sorry to the people who were affected . . . I take responsibility for what happens at my show."[2] While three producers were fired, many heard the apology as hollow and insincere. Effectively DeGeneres attempted to acknowledge the legitimacy of the allegations while keeping the accusations leveled against herself at arm's length and thereby essentially excusing her own actions.

Within our current culture, sincere apologies appear few and far between. What we find more often are overly defensive apologies, apologies that attempt to spin the situation, and hollow apologies. We have many examples of hollow apologies coming from entertainers, politicians, and other

1. Yandoli, "Ellen's 'Be Kind' Talk Show," paragraphs 1, 21; Tsioulcas and Del Barco, "'Ellen' Producers Face," paragraph 1.

2. Komar, "Worst (and Best) Celebrity Apologies," paragraphs 20–22.

public figures.[3] These statements often acknowledge a general wrongdoing or mistake, regularly portrayed as a lapse in judgment. Not only that, instead of apologizing to the person or persons wronged, the apology is made to others who were not involved in or directly hurt by the incident.[4] Connected to this is the often-used phrase, "I apologize if anyone was offended," which moves the spotlight from the perpetrator's objectively wrong action to the subjective response of the one who was wronged. Another common tactic used is distancing language such as, "Mistakes were made," instead of owning the mistake: "It was my mistake. I was wrong."

There is also a commonality in apologizing for the effects of the action rather than the action itself. Former college and NFL football coach Urban Meyer provides a recent example, after video was posted on social media showing a woman who was not his wife dancing provocatively with him. While Meyer called the incident a "stupid mistake," he publicly apologized not for what happened, but for causing a "distraction" to his football team.[5]

Some progress has been made in our culture regarding apologizing, specifically in what are called "'I'm sorry' laws" becoming more prevalent in the United States among the medical community.[6] These laws make allowances to medical professionals to offer condolences to the family of a patient or an apology to a patient or to a patient's family without these expressions or statements being used against them in a subsequent lawsuit. Currently, thirty-nine US states, along with the District of Columbia, have "provisions regarding medical professionals making apologies or sympathetic gestures."[7] While these laws show development in promoting an apologetic society, far more common are the hollow apologies mentioned above that highlight the fact our culture either does not understand what it means to apologize or simply does not care. This gives the church the opportunity to show and live out true biblical repentance, as repentance becomes rediscovered and embraced as a vital part of the mission of the church.

Thus far we have defined repentance and have seen in detail how repentance is a major piece of God's mission in the world, as well as a central component to Jesus' mission as he incarnated and fulfilled the *missio Dei*. As we defined repentance, we saw it requires taking the full biblical witness into account. In doing that, I noted six defining pieces of repentance. Let's mention them here once more:

3. See Garber, "Sorry, Not Sorry."
4. For example, see Stewart, "Mario Batali's Sexual Misconduct," paragraph 5.
5. DiRocco, "Urban Meyer Apologizes Again," paragraphs 3–4.
6. Morton, "Medical Professional Apologies Statutes," paragraphs 1–3.
7. Morton, "Medical Professional Apologies Statutes," paragraph 3.

1. Repentance is a response to God.

2. Repentance brings evidence.

3. Repentance is for everyone.

4. Repentance is for sins.

5. Repentance saves from divine consequences.

6. Repentance occurs in the context of relationships.

There is, however, a seventh piece we have been building toward and waiting to explore. Not only is repentance a central piece to the mission of God and to the mission of Jesus, but repentance is central to the mission of the church. If the American evangelical church desires to follow the example of God and the example of Jesus as it engages in and with the world, then part of that engagement is proclaiming and embodying the message of repentance—the message that God desires for human beings to turn/return to him through the salvific work of Jesus Christ.

The purpose of this present chapter is threefold. First, we see even though repentance is a central piece of the *missio Dei* and the mission of Jesus, a proper understanding of repentance is derelict in the American evangelical church today.[8] Second, we examine the mission of the church, where we discover repentance has not been seen as a part of that mission in its fullest sense. Third, we seek to understand where and how we do see repentance and mission linked in the New Testament.

A CHURCH IN NEED

If we seek a direct answer to the question, "What is the current state of repentance, as it is understood and practiced, in the American evangelical church today?," we won't find a singular answer. One Barna study cited repentance as one of four obstacles people must overcome to "persevere and maximize their connection with God."[9] The study found while 64 percent of "self-identified Christians in the U.S. . . . state that they have confessed their sins to God and asked for His forgiveness," only 3 percent "have come to

8. I am using "evangelical" in the classic way defined by David Bebbington and cited by Sweeney. Bebbington outlines four parts to evangelicalism: "*conversionism*, the belief that lives need to be changed; *activism*, the expression of the gospel in effort; *biblicism*, a particular regard for the Bible, and what be called *crucicentrism*, a stress on the sacrifice of Christ on the cross. Together they form a quadrilateral of priorities that is the basis of Evangelicalism." Sweeney, *American Evangelical Story*, 18. Also see Noll, "Defining Evangelicalism," 20–21.

9. Barna Group, "Self-Described Christians," paragraphs 3, 5.

the final stops on the transformational journey—the places where they have surrendered control of their life to God, submitted to his will for their life, and devoted themselves to loving and serving God and other people."[10] This is how Barna defines true repentance. Additionally, when we examine two prominent and contemporary issues, we see the church is not clear on the meaning, purpose, and mission of repentance. We begin with our understanding of sin and move to the way repentance has become meshed with unhealthy feelings of guilt and shame.

Within our current culture, many are quick to label certain actions, beliefs, and attitudes as "sin." Whether it is the perception of white privilege, the teaching of critical race theory, humanity's treatment of the environment, or the teaching of another pastor with which they don't agree, our culture is quick to label these (and many other things) as "sin" and thus issue calls to repentance. The recent issues surrounding white privilege, critical race theory, and racism have seen declarations of what defines sin and calls for repentance being needed from people in every aspect of society. We see one example of this dynamic in the way two Southern Baptist groups have chosen to address the issue of racism in our society and how these two groups understand as the sin of racism. While an open letter from the six presidents of Southern Baptist seminaries condemns racism, it also declares, "Critical Race Theory, Intersectionality, and any version of Critical Theory [as] incompatible with the Baptist Faith & Message."[11] In a later comment, one seminary president called these pieces part of an "unbiblical ideology."[12] While the word "sin" is not explicitly used, the implication is certainly there.

On the other side of the issue, some Black pastors and Black churches have decided to disassociate from the Southern Baptist Convention over these same issues. These pastors see such statements as those made by the seminary presidents as a way to effectively stop any real and meaningful change within the practical life and theology of the denomination.[13] Meanwhile, some white and Black leaders have come together in "opposition to any movement in the SBC that seeks to distract from racial reconciliation through the gospel," calling a denial of systemic injustice the same as ignoring "the effects of sin" on "individuals, societies, and institutions."[14] In response, these leaders call for "collective repentance," saying, "We believe God is calling us to repentance as individuals and as a convention of

---

10. Barna Group, "Self-Described Christians," paragraph 5.

11. Schroeder, "Seminary Presidents Declare CRT Incompatible," paragraph 2.

12. Schroeder, "Seminary presidents Declare CRT Incompatible," paragraph 14.

13. See Bailey and Boorstein, "Several Black Pastors Break."

14. "Statement on Justice, Repentance, and the SBC," paragraph 11.

churches."[15] These two groups are both attempting to address the racism still occurring in American society today; however, whereas one sees certain means of addressing the issue as sinful, the other views a lack of addressing the issue as sinful. Where, then, does repentance need to take place?

It is hard to follow issues like these and not become confused or even indifferent. The illustration above is simply one example of the nuance and complexity we encounter when we try to define sin and call for repentance. Does that mean, however, it is better not to try to define sin or call for repentance at all? Certainly not. We have already noted how the Old Testament prophets mention specific sins. One of the reasons Jesus came was to call sinners. Additionally, the New Testament contains several lists of sinful behaviors that Christians are to remove from their lives (Rom 1:29–32; Gal 5:19–21; Col 3:5–9). Such sinful behaviors cause us to turn away from God, and are effects of a life turned away from God. The example of Jesus and the example of the Bible is to call men and women to turn from sin.

But what we see in our world today, and what we saw in the example of the SBC above, is finger-pointing on many levels and with almost every issue. One group can call out the sin of sexual immorality in unmarried couples living together and call them to repentance, while another points the finger at the sin of economic injustice that makes it all but impossible for a single income to live in many cities, contributing to cohabitation to avoid living in poverty, which in turn leads to calls for wage-setting corporate CEOs and industry leaders to repent. Accusations of sin, and thus the need to repent, fly from the political left to the political right—and back. From religious conservatives to religious liberals—and back. They fly across economic, racial, ethnic, educational lines. It seems everyone can accuse someone else of sin and then demand their repentance.

In one way this actually highlights the words of Scripture, like Romans 3:23, but in another way this inoculates us to the very idea of sin and therefore the need to repent. Instead of seeing sin as something to avoid, it "has been caricatured, a tool for advertisers to suggest that a product is good and pleasurable . . . [it] is now part and parcel of the human desire that drives consumerist mentalities."[16] It's no wonder that our culture doesn't know how to address mistakes; thus the hollow apologies we saw above.

What we do see as sin is not what others define as wrong, unethical, or immoral, but rather what we ourselves define as sin—which consists only of when we fail to be true to ourselves and fail to live up to or live by our own

---

15. "Statement on Justice, Repentance, and the SBC," paragraphs 14, 12.

16. Mann, *Atonement*, 14.

moral code.[17] Returning to an idea we introduced in chapter 3, according to David Bentley Hart, the essence of modernity is freedom; he calls it "modernity's central 'idea.'"[18] However, whereas Christian freedom consists of the freedom to choose what is good, true, and beautiful, modernity has projected a freedom that gives "a sense of liberty from arbitrary authority, and of limitless inner possibilities, and of profound personal dignity."[19] Within our modern society, then, freedom is found in individual choice, a choice made without influence or restraint. It is the ability itself to choose what is good, true, and beautiful—not the result or outcome of the choice. Consequently, our society is full of ethical contradictions.[20] We often fail to notice these contradictions in ourselves because what matters most is the choice. We often easily spot the same contradictions in others. Thus, we have come to live in a strange world where everything and nothing is sin at the same time, and therefore repentance means almost nothing at all. Or if repentance is referenced, it seems like an antiquated or even a confusing concept.

As we saw in the last chapter, repentance defines a central piece of God's mission as revealed throughout the Old Testament and in Jesus. In addition, repentance is multifaceted, as we have seen in detail. However, for many Christians this multifaceted explanation of repentance is not what directly comes into their minds when they read or hear the term. Within the minds, and unfortunately the experiences, of many Christians is the mistake of equating repentance with shame and guilt.[21] The paradigm learned by

17. Mann says, "If sin exists at all, we encounter it only when we fail to devote ourselves to the project of self-realization. Our pursuit of self-awareness, self-esteem, wholeness, and well-being is paramount. To be *self-centered* is a twenty-first-century virtue, for no Other/other can be trusted to bring the good life we crave. One who fails at *project-self* (a failure defined by the individual's own ideas of success based upon culture and social influences) must gaze into the mirror and confess: 'Against you alone have I sinned.'" Mann, *Atonement*, 17.

18. Hart, *Atheist Delusions*, 24.

19. Hart, *Atheist Delusions*, 22.

20. Hart writes, "It is rare, however, that we are able to impose anything like a coherent pattern upon the somewhat haphazard collection of principles and practices by which we do this [try to live ethically]. Our ethics, especially, tends to be something of a continuous improvisation or bricolage: we assemble fragments of traditions we half remember, gather ethical maxims almost at random from the surrounding culture, attempt to find inner equilibrium between tolerance and conviction, and so on, until we have knit together something like a code, suited to our needs, temperaments, capacities, and imaginations." Hart, *Atheist Delusions*, 23.

21. Stump speaks to guilt, shame, and repentance. For example, she writes, "We are accustomed to think of the antidote to guilt as repentance (or perhaps repentance and making amends) on the part of the guilty person, and forgiveness on the part of the relevant others." She implies that repentance cannot serve as the antidote to guilt, that only occurs through atonement. Stump, *Atonement*, 18.

many Christians is if one sins (either by commission or omission), entertains sinful thoughts or attitudes, or holds wrong beliefs, then one must repent—which, in this guilt and shame paradigm, means 1) recognizing the wrong; 2) feeling shame, guilt, remorse, or contrition about it; and 3) vowing not to do it again.

R. C. Sproul comes close to this paradigm when he writes that repentance "contains the idea of *ruing*."[22] "Rue" means "to regret a particular action. It carries with it not only an intellectual assessment but also an emotional or visceral response. The feeling most often associated with repentance in Scripture is that of remorse, regret, and a sense of sorrow for having acted a particular way."[23] My issue with Sproul here is that godly regret and remorse can too easily turn to ungodly shame and guilt. Instead of understanding repentance as returning to relationship with God through God's kindness (Rom 2:4), it becomes a task demanded by a deity who uses guilt and shame to manipulate people into doing one action over another. That is not repentance as we have been studying it.

Thus, many hide from repentance. Either it becomes avoided because of the guilt and shame associated with it or it becomes a mere hollow apology to God. This is how I understood repentance before I began to suspect there was more to it than I had realized or had been taught. There was an angst that repentance had to be done correctly, with the right amount of guilt and shame, otherwise it was not sincere and would not be honored by God. Under my previous understanding, Jesus' call to "Repent, for the kingdom of heaven is at hand" (Matt 4:17) was ominous and foreboding. It was not an invitation, made in love and grace, to turn back into relationship and realign oneself with God. I was, as many Christians are, stuck in guilt and shame because I hadn't come to understand the fullness of repentance.

Also included in the meaning of repentance for many Christians is repentance as a response to the fear of punishment.[24] While recognizing sin produces consequences, including divine consequences, can lead one to repent, merely repenting to avoid punishment alone does not do justice to the complexity and beauty of repentance. While this is problematic, more

22. Sproul. *What Is Repentance?*, 3.

23. Sproul, *What Is Repentance?*, 3.

24. Chamberlain writes, "In the Protestant Church, for instance, repentance has been almost exclusively associated with an emotional crisis of sorrow for sin and fear of punishment. There has developed in the minds of our more intelligent people a mental resistance to the idea of repentance as they have heard it preached. The instinct back of this reaction is essentially sound. The popular evangelist has so frequently used the fear of punishment to precipitate this crisis, that, in the minds of many, the word repent veritably smells of fire and brimstone." Chamberlain, *Meaning of Repentance*, 18–19.

issues arise from repentance being seen as saying, "Oops, I'm sorry," to God in what amounts to a hollow apology.

The misunderstanding of repentance can also be seen in Christian books. Often the theme of repentance is simply a command from the author to repent from a certain sin, a certain attitude, or a certain understanding of God. I have no doubt many pastors issue similar calls to repent of one thing or another in sermons each and every Sunday. Indeed, a call to turn/return to God should be on the lips of pastors; however, just as with some authors, when pastors mention repentance, they often assume their congregants know what repentance is and what it means. But do they? Do we?

Many problems exist with this popular paradigm of repentance as we have been discussing it. Central to these problems is that this paradigm does not fit the biblical witness that we spent the last chapter exploring. Within the experience of Christians, and within the culture, repentance has become either a way to deal with guilt and shame or an apology to God for a vague wrongdoing—in a similar way to the hollow apologies of public figures in our culture today. But, as we have seen, there is more to repentance. It is bigger than we have probably ever understood before. Repentance isn't a way for God to guilt us and shame us; repentance itself is a grace from God.[25] Repentance is not merely our apology to God or a "get out of jail free" card from some divine punishment; it is an aspect of God's love, forgiveness, and mercy. Part of the way repentance is bigger is that we discover repentance is central to the mission of the church.

Before moving on to show how repentance was a central message within the early church and in the writings of the apostle Paul, let's briefly define "church" and what its mission is.

THE CHURCH AND ITS MISSION

As pastors and church leaders, our ministries, and much of our lives, are centered around the church and its ministries. We understand the church exists for worship, fellowship, and evangelism, but have we ever stopped to ask: What is the church? What is its mission?

Within Scripture, we see the church called a "temple," a "body," a "bride," a "family," a "house," and more. Paul S. Minear identifies no less than ninety-six different images used in the New Testament to describe or define the church.[26] In other words, God has given us a ubiquity of metaphors to

25. Watson opens his book by saying, "Reader, the two great graces essential to a saint in this life, are faith and repentance." Watson, *Doctrine of Repentance*, 1.

26. See Minear, *Images of the Church*.

describe it. As we define what the church is, we must begin by asking: is the church anything more than a group of people gathered together either in a specific place or through the use of technology? In a merely human or physical sense, the answer is no, though the act of gathering together is one aspect of the church.

This quality of the church gained a new level of visibility during the COVID-19 pandemic. Throughout the pandemic, many churches could not meet in person for a time and instead relied upon technology to conduct church services. Throughout the weeks or months of online meetings, churches were reminded once again that the church is more than a building; the church is a people. And when the people of the church meet together, it is a group of people choosing to meet together in the name of Jesus Christ. Thus, a relational aspect is foundational to the meaning of the church. Additionally, meeting together in the name of Jesus Christ makes the church more than something human or physical, but spiritual as well.

Different church traditions understand the makeup and character of the church in different ways. Veli-Matti Kärkkäinen points out within Eastern Orthodoxy, the church is seen as being in the image of the Trinity, and the heart of the church is the Eucharist.[27] He writes of the Eastern Orthodox perspective, "The church makes the Eucharist, and the Eucharist makes the church."[28] Within the Roman Catholic tradition, the church is the gathering of God's people, under the authority of bishops and pastors, where the sacraments are administered.[29] John Calvin understood the church to be the visible community of the elect,[30] while in Free churches, including Baptists, the church consists of believers in Jesus Christ. The church is constituted by "those who are truly converted, who are born from above of God, who are of a regenerate mind by the operation of the Holy Spirit through the hearing of the Word of God, and have become the children of God," and are thus recognizable to each other.[31] Essential within the Free or Believers' churches is the priesthood of all believers, which articulates the belief that all believers have access to God without the need of any human mediator, such as a priest or pope.[32] Examining these church traditions underscores the two foundational elements of the church mentioned above. First, the church is the people of God, gathered for the purpose of worship and the

27. Kärkkäinen, *Ecclesiology*, 19, 21.

28. Kärkkäinen, *Ecclesiology*, 21.

29. Kärkkäinen, *Ecclesiology*, 29.

30. Kärkkäinen, *Ecclesiology*, 51–52.

31. Kärkkäinen, *Ecclesiology*, 62.

32. Kärkkäinen, *Ecclesiology*, 65.

sacraments, yet the church does not cease to exist when the people of God are not gathered together. Second, the church is more than physical; it is spiritual—whether the spiritual focus is the Eucharist, the sacraments, or the Word of God.

These help us define what constitutes the church, but we also want to know: what is the mission of the church?

For our purposes, three aspects of the church's mission are helpful to discuss. First, the church's mission is a continuation of Jesus' own mission, because the church belongs to Jesus. Jürgen Moltmann, in the opening chapter of *The Church in the Power of the Spirit*, perceptively says of the church, "It stands for God to the world, and it stands for the world before God."[33] By this Moltmann means the church "will give an account of itself at all times" to God while it will also "render an account to men about the commission implicit in its faith and the way it is fulfilling its mission."[34] The mission of the church is so vital both God and the world will hold the church to account for the way it fulfills its mission in the world. The church connects God and the world in and through Jesus, because the church is first and foremost the church of Jesus Christ, as Moltmann writes, "But Christ is his church's foundation, its power and its hope."[35] For Moltmann, "the way one thinks about Christ is also the way one thinks about the church."[36] The church can only be viewed, understood, and defined in light of Jesus Christ and who he was and what he did. Thus, for the church to be the church, it must "be drawn into [Jesus'] mission: the messianic liberation of those who are imprisoned in its present day."[37] The messianic liberation that occurs in Jesus is both Christ's mission and the mission of the church, as part of God's mission: "If the church sees itself to be sent in the same framework as the Father's sending of the Son and the Holy Spirit, then it also sees itself in the framework of God's history with the world and discovers its place and function within this history."[38] Therefore, the church is defined by the way it joins in with the mission of Jesus, which, as we have seen, is the incarnation and fulfillment of the *missio Dei*.

Edward L. Smither essentially echoes Moltmann, saying, "I am persuaded that Christian mission flows from the mission of God (*missio Dei*) as 'God is the one who initiates and sustains mission.' That is God is a

33. Moltmann, *Church in the Power*, 1.

34. Moltmann, *Church in the Power*, 1.

35. Moltmann, *Church in the Power*, 5.

36. Moltmann, *Church in the Power*, 66.

37. Moltmann, *Church in the Power*, 68.

38. Moltmann, *Church in the Power*, 11.

missionary God, and he invites the church to participate in his redemptive work among the nations."[39] Craig Ott adds his voice in agreement as well. He writes:

> There may be different ways to formulate a mission statement with various nuances and emphases. But *God* has created the church and commissioned the church for *his* purposes. That calling is spelled out for us in the Scriptures, and our role as his people is to clearly discern that calling. Time and again we must recalibrate our understanding of the church, examine the investment of our energies, and purify our motives so as to maintain alignment with that mission, God's own mission.[40]

Second, the church's mission is one of transformation. Ott goes on to define the mission of the church, saying the church is "to glorify God by multiplying transformational churches among all people."[41] This transformation "always has to do with change *from* something *to* something else, whereby the change is substantive and affecting the very essence or nature of the object."[42] Ott defines this transformation as *metamorphoō* in Greek; however, it also sounds very similar to what we have discovered as the meaning of *metanoia*—repentance. Ott continues by noting, "Scripture describes many aspects of dramatic change in lives and communities without using a specific word that could be translated as 'transform' or 'transformation.'"[43] Again, as we have examined, one word or theme used to describe a dramatic change in lives and communities is *metanoia*, repentance.

While Ott does not connect the theme of change, or "transformation" as he calls it, in the church to repentance, Scott Sunquist does, saying, "Believers are unified by the confession of Jesus Christ through repentance and the experience of forgiveness: this is the foundation of Christian community."[44] For Sunquist repentance and forgiveness constitute one piece that unifies the community of believers into the church.[45] The church then

---

39. Smither, *Mission in the Early Church*, 2.

40. Ott, *Church on Mission*, 2. Emphasis original.

41. Ott, *Church on Mission*, 2.

42. Ott, *Church on Mission*, 5. Emphasis original.

43. Ott, *Church on Mission*, 6.

44. Sunquist, *Understanding Christian Mission*, 288. Boda acknowledges that "repentance is the key human response [to Jesus] on the lips of the early preachers of the church in the book of Acts," but he stops short of emphasizing this response and transformation as a major mission of the church, either in Acts or for today. Boda, *Return to Me*, 165.

45. Sunquist, *Understanding Christian Mission*, 289.

is "a gathering of those who have repented and been forgiven."[46] It is also repentance that breaks down barriers and leads to the change in lives and communities that Ott identifies above.[47]

Gordon T. Smith links repentance with confession of sins. He notes times of confession are largely missing from evangelical worship today.[48] Historically, however, confession of sins was a central component to evangelicalism—from Luther, to Calvin, to the Puritans and John Wesley.[49] Smith concludes by saying, in part, "The call to repentance is inherent in the gospel; the gospel is not preached unless there is a call for repentance."[50] If part of the gospel is the message that returning to God is possible through the life, death, and resurrection of Jesus, and if preaching the gospel is part of the church's mission, then repentance is part of the mission of the church. Smith lays the foundation for this conclusion, though he does not make the connection himself.

Similarly, Sunquist affirms repentance is one foundational aspect to Christian mission and even to our participation in the *missio Dei*;[51] however, when it comes to identifying repentance as part of the mission of the church, he only emphasizes its place in individual spiritual formation.[52] He identifies repentance as an "element of spiritual formation for mission" but doesn't connect repentance to the active mission of the church. While Sunquist, in an otherwise superb book, rightfully sees how repentance leads us to humility and to recognize our need for forgiveness, he misses the connection of repentance within the mission of God and the church in the way that I am articulating; namely, repentance should be one of the messages of the church as it fulfills its mission in the world.

He agrees with the other theologians we have cited who understand the mission of the church in light of God's mission in the world. Sunquist defines the two basic purposes of the church as being worship and mission (witness).[53] The mission the church is called to is the mission of Jesus Christ to the nations, which entails "loving, healing, including, proclaiming, and reconciling."[54] Central to Jesus' mission, and part of the way his "loving,

---

46. Sunquist, *Understanding Christian Mission*, 288.

47. Sunquist, *Understanding Christian Mission*, 289–290.

48. G. T. Smith, "Penitential," 268.

49. G. T. Smith, "Penitential," 270–71.

50. G. T. Smith, "Penitential," 281.

51. Sunquist, *Understanding Christian Mission*, 400.

52. Sunquist, *Understanding Christian Mission*, 400.

53. Sunquist, *Understanding Christian Mission*, 281.

54. Sunquist, *Understanding Christian Mission*, 282.

healing, including, proclaiming, and reconciling" are seen, is his incarnation and fulfillment of God's mission of repentance.[55]

Third, the church has the mission to announce and live out something new. Looking at mission from a slightly different perspective, Lesslie Newbigin invites us to understand the beginning of mission as being rooted in "the presence of a new reality."[56] Through the power of the Holy Spirit a new reality has come, a reality where humans, in their weakness, recognize "the presence and power of God."[57] For Newbigin the mission of the church is to share in Jesus' weaknesses, suffering, and rejection, and through that to share in Christ's life, power, and triumph in the Holy Spirit.[58] As the church lives in this story, it is then able to call the world to turn to God in faith and enter into this new reality and enter into God's ultimate history.[59] This describes repentance.[60] This link between repentance and the new reality inaugurated by God through Jesus Christ, as God moves all creation toward his ultimate ends, is the topic of the next chapter.

What we see of these authors and theologians is they agree the church must be defined by its mission and they agree the mission of the church is the extension of the mission of God. In sum, the mission of God cannot be separated from the mission of the church. They are one and the same and contain the same elements, one of those being repentance and proclaiming that God, in Jesus, has made a way for human beings to turn/return and be in relationship with him.

55. Newbigin also emphasizes reconciliation within God's mission. He says the "biblical story" gives a "clear vision of the goal of history—namely the reconciliation of all things with Christ as Head—and the assurance that this goal will be reached." Reconciliation, by definition, involves the coming together or reuniting of something separated. Repentance certainly must be included within the practical outworking of reconciling. Repentance is the turning back that must occur before the reconciliation can take place. Newbigin, *Gospel in a Pluralist Society*, 101.

56. Newbigin, *Gospel in a Pluralist Society*, 119.

57. Newbigin, *Gospel in a Pluralist Society*, 119.

58. Newbigin, *Gospel in a Pluralist Society*, 120–22.

59. Newbigin, *Gospel in a Pluralist Society*, 123–25, 133. Here Newbigin describes the new reality in Jesus: "What is this new reality? In the Gospels the new reality is the presence of Jesus himself. He is here. In him the kingdom of God has come near so that it now confronts men and women with its reality and requires them either to be so radically turned around that they recognize the truth and believe, or else to continue on their way facing in the wrong direction and pursuing that which is not God's kingdom." *Gospel in a Pluralist Society*, 133.

60. Newbigin, *Gospel in a Pluralist Society*, 117. Newbigin does cite repentance as a prerequisite to mission, but he does not emphasize repentance directly as being a part of the mission of the church going forward, however, it's clear that it is.

REPENTANCE AND MISSION IN ACTS AND PAUL

In Luke's gospel, as Jesus is preparing to ascend to the Father after the resurrection, he gives his disciples their mission. Just as I argued that repentance is one piece, but a central piece, of the *missio Dei* and one central piece of Jesus' mission, here I am not arguing there are no other pieces to the church's mission; there are. I am arguing repentance is, in fact, a central piece of the church's mission. Additionally, the church's mission is linked to Jesus' mission and God's mission, as Jesus says in John 20:21, "Peace be with you; as the Father has sent Me, I also send you." We find another link between Jesus' mission and that of his followers in Mark 6:7–13. There Jesus sends out his disciples for ministry, and "they went out and preached that men should repent" (6:12). In Matthew's account, more attention is given to Jesus' instructions. There we find the disciples should preach about the kingdom of heaven (kingdom of God) as Jesus himself preached. Furthermore, Jesus instructs them, saying they are to become like him, not only in enduring persecution, but also, as is implied, in his mission (Matt 10:24–25).

Part of Jesus' explanation for his death and resurrection and part of the mission of his followers is the message of the Scriptures: "That the Christ would suffer and rise again from the dead the third day, and that repentance for forgiveness of sins would be proclaimed in His name to all the nations, beginning from Jerusalem" (Luke 24:46–47).[61] Then Jesus tells them they are "witnesses" of these things and says they are to remain in Jerusalem until the Holy Spirit comes upon them (24:48–49). Of course, these same themes comprise Jesus' mission call in Acts 1:1–8. There Jesus speaks again of the coming Holy Spirit and calls his followers to be witnesses of him to the whole world—beginning in Jerusalem (1:8). As Acts comes to a close, we find Paul's testimony before King Agrippa in Acts 26, where Paul declares the mission of Acts 1:8 is in the process of being accomplished:

> "So, King Agrippa, I did not prove disobedient to the heavenly vision, but kept declaring both to those of Damascus first, and also at Jerusalem and then throughout all the region of Judea, and even to the Gentiles, that they should repent and turn to God, performing deeds appropriate to repentance." (Acts 26:19–20)

Paul declares he has carried out the mission given to him—the same mission given to the apostles and to the church—by preaching repentance to both Jews and Gentiles, starting in Jerusalem and extending through the

---

61. See Nave, "'Repent, for the Kingdom,'" 97.

entire Gentile world.[62] As we saw, Jesus' commission in the conclusion of Luke includes repentance. By linking witness in Luke 24:48 and preaching repentance in Luke 24:47 to being witnesses in Acts 1:8, surely one aspect of being a witness is proclaiming repentance for forgiveness of sins in Jesus' name. Finally, as Acts closes, Paul testifies he has preached repentance, and thus he has fulfilled his divine mandate to "open their [Jews and Gentiles] eyes so that they may turn from darkness to light and from the dominion of Satan to God, that they may receive forgiveness of sin and an inheritance among those who have been sanctified by faith" (26:18). As Luke writes Luke–Acts, he is obviously mentioning repentance at these points to highlight the importance of repentance within the mission of the early church.

Metanoia and *metanoeo* are used a total of eleven times throughout Acts.[63] Of these eleven uses, four are by Peter and one is by the church in Jerusalem. The other six uses are by Paul as he travels, proclaiming the gospel and planting churches. Additionally, Acts contains eight uses of *epistrephó*, turn. Altogether, the theme of turning or returning to God, based on these Greek words alone, is seen nineteen times throughout Acts. When Guy D. Nave Jr. comes to Acts, he correctly perceives Acts as the continuation of the narrative and theology of Luke. Nave understands that "in Luke–Acts the extension of salvation to and the inclusion of all people within the family of God represents the plan of God. Furthermore, the human response of repentance to the offer of salvation comprises a vital part of that plan."[64] We have noted the universality of repentance as one aspect of God's plan and Jesus' mission, while Nave understands it as the central component of Luke–Acts. Nevertheless, Nave acknowledges, "Without a doubt, according to Luke-Acts, repentance is part of the plan of God."[65] The question is: is repentance part of God's plan *for the church*?

Nave certainly understands repentance as being part of Jesus' commission to his disciples in Luke before the work of the church begins in

---

62. Nave comments, "Through Paul's preaching of repentance to Jews in Damascus, Jerusalem and throughout Judea, as well as to Gentiles everywhere, God's demand for universal repentance is being accomplished." Nave, *Repentance in Luke–Acts*, 220. Nave goes on to note that Paul's testimony includes two aspects that are universal to repentance, which we have already noted. First, repentance is for the forgiveness of sins. Second, repentance brings evidence. Nave, however, does not address repentance in Acts or in Paul in connection to the mission of the church.

63. Of the fifty-six uses of *metanoia* and *metanoeo* in the New Testament, twenty-five come in Luke–Acts. Within Acts the words are found in 2:38; 3:19; 5:31; 8:22; 11:18; 13:24; 17:30–31; 19:4; 20:21; 26:20 (in both noun and verb form).

64. Nave, *Repentance in Luke–Acts*, 29.

65. Nave, *Repentance in Luke–Acts*, 38.

Acts.[66] Additionally, Nave recognizes repentance as one of the emphases of Peter's preaching. However, Nave's objective is to survey a biblical theology of repentance, noting where and how repentance is used in the narratives of Luke and Acts, and not a full examination of repentance and mission as we are doing here. Nave does argue repentance was central in the mission of the early church to the Gentiles, and was part of what helped establish a "community composed of all people"—two propositions with which I agree.[67] However, we see something else is occurring within the turning theme in Acts as well.

What we find in examining the theme of repentance and turning in Acts is the preaching of the gospel, the formation of the church, and the expansion of the church throughout the world. What we find is mission. We find repentance being vital to the making of the people of God—the church—and the moving of the people of God into the mission of God. The pervasiveness of turning language in Acts indicates repentance it is, in fact, a major theme in Acts and a major part of the mission of the church. To show the seventh defining element of repentance, that repentance is central to the mission of the church, let's examine three overlapping pieces in light of the mission of the church.

1. Repentance in the Church Is a Response to God

As we saw, Jesus teaches his disciples the Scriptures foretold of his mission, passion, resurrection *and* says repentance in his name would be proclaimed to the nations (Luke 24:46–47). Within the preaching of Peter and Paul, Jesus' words are proven true. As Peter preaches on Pentecost in Acts 2, he explains the person and message of Jesus using the Old Testament Scriptures as a guide. When Peter's audience asks, "What shall we do?," Peter replies, "Repent, and each of you be baptized in the name of Jesus Christ for the forgiveness of your sins; and you will receive the gift of the Holy Spirit" (Acts 2:37–38). As a response to what God has done in Jesus, Peter calls on his listeners to turn/return to God. Their repentance is not merely changing their minds about Jesus.[68] Rather, it is an invitation to turn back to God in a sinless relationship. The forgiveness offered by God is enough even to cover the murder of his Son.[69]

66. Nave, *Repentance in Luke–Acts*, 194.

67. Nave, *Repentance in Luke–Acts*, 220–21.

68. Nave, "'Repent, for the Kingdom,'" 98; Nave, *Repentance in Luke–Acts*, 224.

69. Ovey, *Feasts of Repentance*, 42.

We find a similar call to repent in Peter's second sermon, in Acts 3. There Peter calls on his listeners to "repent and return, so that your sins may be wiped away, in order that times of refreshing may come from the presence of the Lord" (3:19). Michael J. Ovey rightly notes by calling the people to repentance and turning, Peter implies the people have turned away from God but turning back is possible.[70] We see repentance is a response to what God has done in Jesus Christ. Yet it is also for sin, including the sin of giving over Jesus to be crucified.[71]

Additionally, and the point of our discussion, something has been missed in the way others have understood repentance in Acts, namely, the context of Peter's sermons. At the end of Acts 2, after Peter's first sermon, we find the first description of the church in verses 43–47. Similarly, after Peter's second sermon and the following story of his arrest in the temple, we find the second description of the church in 3:32–35. Finally, when Peter is before the Jewish Council in Acts 5, he again proclaims that the response to God's actions is repentance for the forgiveness of sins. As with Peter's other appeals for repentance, this comes right in the middle of descriptions and stories of the church in Acts 5–6. Thus, as we follow the theme of repentance within Peter's sermons, we are meant to understand repentance as a foundational piece of the formation of the church. This continues throughout Acts as well. For example, when Christians begin preaching in Antioch in Acts 11, the response to their message includes "a large number who believed turned [*epestrepsen*, from the Greek *epistrephó*] to the Lord" (11:21). It is then the church in Antioch is formed.

As the church is established in the opening chapters of Acts, repentance is integral to its message and mission. At every opportunity, Peter is preaching about who Jesus is and what God has done in Jesus, and then he is calling on his listeners to repent. When men and women turn toward God and away from sin, when they return to a relationship with God through the forgiveness of sins, the result is the building and growth of the church. Worship, fellowship, and evangelism all originate in the turning of men and women toward God. This is not equating repentance with conversion but, as we saw above, they are two sides of the same coin. We can even read the story of Ananias and Sapphira in Acts 5 as a story about the lack of repentance and its seriousness within the church and the necessity of repentance for continuing to carry out the mission of the church, namely, to call men and women to turn to God.

70. Ovey, *Feasts of Repentance*, 44.
71. See Ovey, *Feasts of Repentance*, 42, 43–44.

We already observed how Paul sees repentance as a central piece to his God-given mission to preach the gospel to Jews and Gentiles throughout the whole world. Just as we see in Peter, throughout Acts we find Paul also preaching repentance as the necessary response to what God has done in the work of Jesus. One aspect of Paul's preaching of repentance connects back to the work of John the Baptist (Acts 13:24; 19:4). By referencing John the Baptist and his call for repentance, what is Paul saying?[72] Paul seems to be saying John the Baptist's call to return to God was part of God's plan and preparation for the coming Messiah. This is consistent with Paul's message that the gospel is first for Jews—they were privileged to have an advanced announcement—since John the Baptist preached almost exclusively to Jews. Additionally, Paul highlights the singularity of God's mission: just as we saw the prophets preach repentance, John the Baptist also preached repentance, as did Jesus, and now repentance is the message and mission of the church as it is preached in Jesus' name.

We need to reevaluate how we are calling men and women to respond to what God has done in Jesus. Yes, the early church called men and women to believe and to be saved, but the early church also called men and women to repent—to turn or turn back to God and be realigned with him and in relationship to him. It was a central piece of the message and the mission of the early church. It must be rediscovered as a central piece of the church's mission today as well.

As our churches attempt to respond to many of the issues we're facing in today's world, including racial relations, toxic masculinity, the #MeToo movement, and transgenderism, not to mention the temptations and sins that we face on a daily basis, our message cannot be, "Change," "Conform," "Do," "Stop." Rather, our message is, "Repent and turn/return to God; come back into relationship with him." We preach repentance, not in a way that perpetuates the cycle of guilt and shame, but rather as a response to what God has done in Jesus. We preach repentance as an invitation to realign our whole being with God in a life-changing and life-giving way.

What we see in Acts is that this message is a central piece of God's mission for the church. The reason is because the response we call for will become the foundation the church is built on. If we are not seeing our churches act in the way we see the church does in Acts, part of the reason may be we are not inviting people into the fullness of repentance as we have

---

72. Nave says just as John the Baptist "demanded a change of thinking among the Jewish people in order that they might be able to receive the teachings and believe in the person of Jesus," so Paul is preaching "a similar change of thinking among the Gentiles regarding their pagan and idolatrous practices." Nave, *Repentance in Luke–Acts*, 216, footnote 323. The problem is that in both Acts 13 and Acts 19, Paul is speaking mostly to Jews.

been exploring. For many it is still seen as related to guilt and shame, not as a foundational action of the church.

2. The Church Calls Everyone to Repent

Continuing and overlapping with number 1 is the invitation to repentance offered to both Jews and Gentiles. In Peter's sermons around Pentecost and Paul's teaching elsewhere, especially in Pisidian Antioch, the message is: "Because of what God has done in Jesus, turning to God for the forgiveness of sin is available to all through faith." This message also extends to the Gentiles.

When Paul preaches to Gentiles in Athens and calls them to repentance in Acts 17, he does not, as Nave suggests, merely appeal to the Athenians to change their minds about their idolatry.[73] Certainly turning to God, as we have seen, includes turning away from idols and false gods. Paul's message is not one of condemnation for the idolatry of the Athenians; rather Paul commends their spirituality and their God-given desire to seek for God (17:27). Yes, mankind previously sought for God in ignorance, but now God is declaring all people can turn to him (17:30). We come to a similar conclusion when we examine Paul's message in Lystra in Acts 14. While Paul does call them to turn from "vain things to a living God" (14:15), the reason for turning is because while God allowed human beings to "go their own ways" (14:16), he always left a "witness" to testify to himself in order that humans might return to him. Truly this is good news. When Paul returns, he appoints elders in every church as their acceptance of his preaching and their repentance led to the formation of a church (Acts 14:21–23).

Likewise, as Paul recounts his ministry in his farewell address in Miletus (Acts 20), Paul declares he "did not shrink from declaring to you publicly and from house to house, solemnly testifying to both Jews and Greeks of repentance toward God and faith in our Lord Jesus Christ" (20:20–21). Paul preaches a singular message, a message applying to both Jews and Gentiles.[74] As Paul tells the Corinthians, he is determined to know only one thing—Jesus Christ and him crucified (1 Cor 2:2). The necessary response to this message, whether for Jews or Gentiles, is a turning to God through faith in Jesus, and the effect is the formation of the church.

73. Nave, *Repentance in Luke–Acts*, 216.

74. Ovey writes, "Paul, then, has one message, which applies to both Jews and Greeks alike." Ovey, *Feasts of Repentance*, 58.

As Paul encourages the leaders of the Ephesian church, he is essentially giving them a "miniature letter" in the form of an oral address.[75] He reminds them of their foundation, repentance and faith in the Lord Jesus Christ, and encourages them to hold fast to this confession even in the midst of persecution and false teaching that is sure to come. Through these teachings and accounts, we find repentance is the foundation of the church. The church is a group of men and women who have repented and found forgiveness of sin in Jesus Christ. This is the message Peter and Paul preach to everyone, Jew and Gentile alike.

The question for us is: are we calling on all people to repent? Does our call include Christians? The commonality between every man and woman is each one needs to turn to God; all people need to repent. All men and women, left to their own devices, will turn to sin and away from God, and each person needs to turn back and realign with God. This happens through repentance and faith in Jesus. However, we can believe in God yet not be aligned with him. Thus, repentance continues throughout and encompasses our whole lives, and, as the church, we never stop preaching the message of repentance.

Søren Kierkegaard, for example, chastised the recently deceased Bishop Mynster, whom others heralded as a "witness to the truth," because Bishop Mynster did not preach repentance, which Kierkegaard called a point "most decisively Christian."[76] Martin Luther also was correct when he proposed in the first of his Ninety-Five Theses, "When our Lord and Master Jesus Christ said, 'Repent', he willed the entire life of believers to be one of repentance."[77] For the church to fulfill its mission, not only do we need to preach repentance for all people, but we need to preach repentance continues for all people, throughout their lives. As faith grows, repentance grows along with it, and when faith and repentance meet, the church can become what it was intended to be.

3. Repentance Continues God's Mission

Third, we find a piece both encapsulating and amplifying the first two pieces we have discussed: the preaching of repentance in the church continues God's mission. Three sections in Acts highlight this point. The first is the response of the church in Jerusalem to the preaching of the gospel to Cornelius and his household in Acts 11. After Peter recounts the events and the

75. Longenecker, *Acts*, 512.

76. Kierkegaard, *Attack upon "Christendom"*, 15–18.

77. Janz, *Reformation Reader*, 88.

activity of God that brought about the salvation of Cornelius, the church affirms "God has granted to the Gentiles also the repentance that leads to life" (11:18). The response of the Jerusalem church is an acknowledgement of God's activity in the expansion of the gospel to the Gentiles. Just as Jesus said, repentance in his name is being proclaimed to all people and expanding to include the ends of the earth. God's mission is continuing in the work and ministry of the church.

The second scene we must mention comes in Acts 15. Paul and Barnabas have returned from their first missionary journey and go to Jerusalem to submit (Gal 2:2) their gospel to the apostles in Jerusalem. After hearing the testimony of Paul about the belief of the Gentiles, including the signs and wonders God performed among them (Acts 15:12), the question of whether Gentiles must obey the Jewish law is debated. The ultimate response, given by James, is "that we [the apostles and the Jerusalem church] not trouble those who are turning to God from among the Gentiles" (15:19).

This judgment by James comes also in response to a threefold argument by Peter concerning God's mission to the Gentiles (Acts 15:6–11). First, God had already given Peter the mission to preach to the Gentiles (as we saw with Cornelius in Acts 10 and including Peter's vision of the sheet); thus Paul's mission to the Gentiles is well within God's own mission as had already been revealed to Peter. Second, the coming of the Holy Spirit upon Gentiles, including the sign of tongues, confirms that faith alone is necessary for salvation. Third, if the Jews could not bear the weight of the law, and if the law did not bring about a cleansing of the heart, why hold Gentiles—who already have shown the signs of salvation—to bear that weight as well?

All of this, Paul and Barnabas' testimony, as well as Peter's defense and the changes in behavior and practice, James labels "turning to God" (Acts 15:19).[78] It involves more than Gentiles changing their mind about God or Jesus, but rather a whole redefinition of relationship with God. The subsequent requests by the Jerusalem church are for the purpose of fellowship between the churches, Jewish and Gentile.[79] Together, because both Jews and Gentiles have turned to God, they are brothers and sisters, together in one church—preaching, teaching, and ministering (Acts 15:23–35).

Third and finally, as already mentioned above, as Paul describes his mission as an apostle and missionary in Acts 26:1–23, he uses the theme

78. This judgment also is informed by Scripture, as we see in Acts 15:16–18. There, James quotes Amos 9:11–12. The quote also makes clear that this returning, rebuilding, and restoring includes the "nations" (Amos 9:12), or Gentiles (Acts 15:17), in fulfillment of God's plan. James reinterprets this text in light of the current ministry and mission of the church.

79. Longenecker, *Acts*, 448.

of repentance. We find references to the theme of repentance in 26:18, 19, and 20. The first of the references comes in the words of Jesus as he commissions Paul. Jesus tells Paul he will be sent to rescue Jews and Gentiles, "to open their eyes so that they may turn from darkness to light and from the dominion of Satan to God, that they may receive forgiveness of sins and an inheritance among those who have been sanctified by faith in Me" (26:18). In the following verses Paul says he has been faithful to this mission and has called all people to "repent and turn to God" and perform "deeds appropriate to repentance" (26:19–20).

It's hard to emphasize enough how central this is as we seek to rediscover repentance as a part of the mission of God. In the same way Jesus calls his disciples to be witnesses in Luke 24 and Acts 1, in Acts 26:16 Jesus calls Paul to be a witness. These calls to be a witness must be seen in relation to one another. Each one builds upon and further explains the others, and in each case, as we've mentioned, repentance stands as a key piece in each commission. Indeed, here in Acts 26 Paul's mission is described as a rescue, a turning (from darkness to light, which is from the dominion of Satan to God), and the forgiveness of sin (which is also an effect of the turning to God). Within the words of Jesus and Paul in Acts 26, we are reminded of passages within Paul's epistles.

While direct references to repentance are rare in Paul's epistles, the theme remains present throughout them.[80] Based on Acts 26, we can understand Colossians, for example, as a commentary on turning to God. We find the same references, as in Acts 26, to rescuing, turning from darkness to God, and finding forgiveness of sins (Col 1:13–14). The reason for this turning is because of Jesus, the image of God, the creator, and the head of the church. From there, Paul emphasizes his ministry and the new people believers become in Jesus (Col 3). Paul's whole letter is built upon the transferring (Colossians) or turning (Acts 26) of a person to God. It's this turning, or repenting, as part of the process of salvation that changes a person from who they were before Jesus to who they are now in Jesus. Paul highlights this and encourages Christians not to turn back to their former ways (Gal 5:16–23; Eph 5:3–21). For Paul turning to God results in a completely new person, and precipitates the fruits of repentance, which, as in John the Baptist's preaching, include new ways to relate to others (Luke 3:8–14; Eph 6:1–9; Col 3:18—4:1).

It seems necessary here to take a brief detour to say a word about repentance and salvation. Is repentance a necessary step within God's work of

---

80. The words "repent" or "repentance" are found in Rom 2:4–5; 2 Cor 7:9–10; 12:21; 2 Tim 2:25. "Turn" (*epistrephó*) is found in 2 Cor 3:16; Gal 4:9; and 1 Thess 1:9. "Regret" or "remorse" (*metameloma*) is found in 2 Cor 7:8.

salvation? While nuances clearly exist, the two basic positions hold either "repentance and [saving] faith are mutually independent" or "repentance and [saving] faith are mutually connected."[81] In the case of the former, repentance is not a step in God's act of salvation; only faith is required. While "in this version faith might be saving . . . it is void of repentance, which gives it at best an anaemic character."[82] Within the case of the latter, faith and repentance are connected in some way; "the connection . . . may be that one produces the other, or that both are sides of the same coin, but the net effect is that in an individual a faithless repentance, or a repentanceless faith, may not be the kind of faith and repentance that lead to justification and forgiveness."[83]

Which of these two camps is correct? Faith and repentance are truly two sides of the same coin.[84] Repentance in salvation is both independent and mutual. We are saved only by grace through faith; by faith, we turn to God and find salvation through God's grace. Part of that faith is in the picture of repentance we have been describing through these chapters, namely, that Jesus' life, death, and resurrection make turning/returning to God possible. "Faith is repentance-shaped and repentance is faith-shaped."[85]

What we conclude from these three sections in Acts is as the church begins and grows, Peter, the apostles, James, and Paul all link the preaching of repentance with their understanding of God's mission and the mission of the church. Preaching repentance and seeing repentance as a response to God and the gospel is what the apostles understand to be central for the church.

Do we see repentance continuing God's mission today? It seems as if our churches are concerned with so many other things—music, aesthetics, technology, politics, culture, none of which are bad in and of themselves—but our mission as a church isn't any of those things. Our mission is to call men and women to turn back to relationship with God and to turn from what they have become and return to who we, as human beings, were created to be—God's own people, in a relationship of love with him. As God's people, who have re-entered that relationship, the mission we have been given is to preach and invite others into what we have in Jesus Christ.

81. Ovey, *Feasts of Repentance*, 104. I have added the descriptor "saving" to faith in these two statements in order to clarify the kind of faith Ovey is referencing.

82. Ovey, *Feasts of Repentance*, 105.

83. Ovey, *Feasts of Repentance*, 105.

84. Ferguson writes, "Faith is trusting in Christ; repentance is turning from sin. They are two sides of the same coin of belonging to Jesus." Ferguson, *Grace of Repentance*, 22.

85. Ovey, *Feasts of Repentance*, 131, quoting John Murray.

CONCLUSION

Looking at this theme as we have, it is not hard to see the connection between repentance and the mission of the church. As we have seen, the church is to continue the mission of God in the world, and that mission includes repentance. As the church forms and expands in the book of Acts, repentance is a dominant theme. Within every step of the church from Jerusalem to Rome, we find repentance being preached. Through repentance we are made into the people of God and we enter into God's mission; a mission that continues the *missio Dei* in the world as we invite men and women to turn to God because of what God has done in Jesus.

If repentance within the book of Acts was such a central component to the establishment of the church, and if repentance helped define the church's mission and contributed to its growth, why has it been neglected as a component of the church's mission today? A large part of the answer goes back to the observations made at the beginning of this chapter. First, as Americans, we live within a culture that has generally forgotten what it means to genuinely admit wrongdoing. This is coupled with our culture's tendency to describe as "sinful" things that are luxurious and elegant, as well as experiences of pleasure ranging from eating chocolate to having sex. Thus, repentance has little context within our current culture. We take up this theme in greater detail in chapter 6. Second, the evangelical church in America too often has become enthralled by calling out sin, both within the church and within the culture. While sin does need to be addressed—again a subject we take up in chapter 6—the eagerness to call out sin (and at times the need for repentance) in others' camps while ignoring sin within one's own camp ends up rendering both calls ineffective and, ultimately, meaningless (see Matt 7:5). In sum, the call to repentance comes as an attack from Christians to the culture or from Christians to other Christians. Thus, repentance becomes rooted in guilt and shame.

Thirdly—and this is the culmination of what we have explored so far—our churches have neglected the *missio Dei*. We have neglected God's mission in the world and have become focused on our own missions. Instead of recognizing God wants all people to turn/return to him, we have become focused on so many other things. What then can we do? The final two chapters explore the answer.

PART 3

6

Turning Toward God's Future

Having explored the meaning of repentance with regard to the mission of God, the mission of Jesus, and the mission of the church, we are able to turn our attention more fully to practice. What does a mission of repentance mean for the church? How can we become agents of turning? Once we have turned and realigned with God, how can we embody God's mission of repentance? As "God works through Jesus" and "Jesus works through his followers," within the community of the church, how do we engage in a ministry of repentance?[1] Just as Paul says we have been reconciled to God in Christ and thus given the ministry of reconciliation as his ambassadors (2 Cor 5:18–20), what would it mean and what would it look like to engage in a ministry of repentance, as we have turned to God in Jesus Christ? If we understood ourselves to be agents, or ambassadors, of repentance, how would we engage in such a mission? These are the questions we want to take up over the closing chapters.

One of the reasons having a defined mission is important is because, as we discussed in chapter 2, it provides a vision of what should be happening, why it should be happening, and where the ultimate end is. Within the previous chapter, we explored the *what* and *why*. Here the purpose is to discover the *where*. The purpose of this chapter is to help us see that repentance turns us toward God's ultimate ends. Repentance leads us, as the church, into an eschatological future. Our closing chapter explores some

---

1. N. T. Wright, *Simply Jesus*, 213.

specific characteristics of individuals and communities needed to carry out this mission of repentance.

When we turn or return, we are not merely returning to what was (i.e., the garden); we are turning toward what is and what will be as God moves all creation toward his ultimate ends. God's intention is not for the world to go back to Eden but rather for a world, a cosmos, where Jesus reigns as the rightful King to bring about "the rescue and renewal of God's creation project."[2] Also, as agents of repentance, we proclaim that the future our hearts so desire is in fact the future God has in store when we turn/return to him. Here we explore three aspects of this future tying into our theme of repentance: the kingdom of God, the transformation that comes by entering the kingdom, and the realization of a new reality that has come and is coming as a result of the kingdom.

These three pieces originate in the work of N. T. Wright, as we briefly noted in chapter 3. He also understands repentance in an eschatological way.[3] As we noted there, for Wright, Jesus' repentance announcement comes within the restoration of Israel amidst the coming of the kingdom,[4] and as Jesus describes the kingdom, as we saw above, he describes something transformed and new. We want to pull together the threads of repentance, mission, and eschatology to see how understanding repentance in the way we have explored can lead the people of God into the mission of God. While we explore some of the current issues affecting the American evangelical church today, we must acknowledge that issues come and go, issues causing authors, bloggers, and editorialists to write change from month to month and from year to year. Our focus is more about the principles than specific examples. Therefore, our focus is somewhat limited to the big ideas, with relevant contemporary issues cited as examples.

WHAT IS ESCHATOLOGY?

First, let's define what we mean by "eschatology." Eschatology is the study of last things, but it is far more than trying to understand or interpret the book of Revelation. Additionally, its definition goes beyond what has come to be defined as the "end times," or ascribing to a premillennial, postmillennial, or amillennial view of the second coming of Christ. So, then, what does eschatology mean? How are we to understand eschatology?

2. N. T. Wright, *Simply Jesus*, 213.

3. N. T. Wright, *Jesus and the Victory*, 251.

4. N. T. Wright, *Jesus and the Victory*, 200.

To begin with, and as Trevin K. Wax notes, eschatology is not exclusively a Christian concept. Rather, it conveys the idea of the future as envisioned by various faith groups or even those without faith.[5] Eschatology is the vision of where the story of the world is going and tells of the world's ultimate ends. For some, the ultimate end of the world resides in technology or in the colonization of Mars and other planets.[6] For others, there is no future for the world and humanity. Instead, they view the world hurtling toward destruction from causes like war, climate change, and natural disasters.[7]

If repentance is tied to the ultimate end, we need to know, what is the Christian vision of the world's future? Where is the story going? What is the world's ultimate end for the believer? For Christians, the world's ultimate future does not culminate in its complete destruction but rather in God's complete and good rule, for God to be "all in all" (1 Cor 15:28). True Christian eschatology, therefore, is not an eschatology of hopelessness. Even if the circumstances of the world seem to be more chaotic, or worse and worsening from our perspective, the world's ultimate end for a believer is a reason for hope.

Lesslie Newbigin helps us see this connection, saying within "the biblical story there is a clear vision of the goal of history—namely the reconciliation of all things with Christ as Head—and the assurance that this goal will be reached. This is what gives . . . the Christian hope."[8] By "hope" Newbigin does not mean simply "things will be what they will be."[9] A biblical hope, as he defines it, anchors the soul in something "utterly reliable"—even if it is hidden or the circumstances seem hopeless. This is because our hope is grounded in the reliability of Jesus Christ as the crucified and resurrected Lord.[10] In other words, because God has fulfilled his promise to raise Jesus from the dead, we can be assured God will fulfill his promises about the world's ultimate future. Repentance is a call to turn to that future.

Thus, our hope for the future is based on history. We see this connection throughout the Old Testament as well. As Israel reflected on its past, it could be certain of its future because of its history. They could be confident

5. Wax, "Eschatological Discipleship," 41–42.

6. See Veith, *Post-Christian*, 256–63.

7. Wax cites, as an example of this view, the novelist Julian Barnes who's "*cosmic* eschatology is that the world is doomed to eventual destruction, and thus, his *collective* eschatology is that all humanity will perish with it, so his *personal* eschatology is that no hope exists for life after death." Wax, "Eschatological Discipleship," 43.

8. Newbigin, *Gospel in a Pluralist Society*, 101.

9. Newbigin, *Gospel in a Pluralist Society*, 101.

10. Newbigin, *Gospel in a Pluralist Society*, 101.

that God would see them through the darkness of their current situation because God saw them through previous dark times. Our hope in God's complete lordship and the reconciliation of all things to himself is reliable because we also know the ways God has worked in the past and we trust God will continue in that work in the future.

It seems likely that Newbigin's eschatology of hope was influenced, at least in part, by Jürgen Moltmann's *Theology of Hope*. Within this work, Moltmann defines eschatology as "the doctrine of the Christian hope."[11] Thus, "eschatology cannot really be only a part of Christian doctrine. Rather, the eschatological outlook is characteristic of all Christian proclamation, of every Christian experience and of the whole Church."[12] Moltmann sees Christianity through the lens of eschatology, as eschatology involves both hope and promise, and the assured hope God will do what he has promised.[13] As with Newbigin, the hope and promise are grounded in the work, including the death and resurrection, of Jesus. Because Jesus has been raised, all of God's promises are fulfilled in him; "they have become an eschatological certainty in Christ, by being liberated and validated, made unconditional and universal."[14] In repentance we turn to God and become aligned with him to see his promises fulfilled, as he brings about his ultimate ends.

We must also understand eschatology as the complete and irrevocable reversal of the fall. As we saw in chapter 2, sin led to Adam and Eve's expulsion from the garden. Humans turned away from God and yet God turned toward them. God made a covenant with Abraham, which included the promise of a land and thus a reversal of Eden on a small scale. God, however, has a much bigger plan and that was and is the redemption of all creation, inaugurated in Jesus' ministry, death, and resurrection, and culminating in Jesus' second coming. N. T. Wright summarizes this eschatological reversal and the redemption of creation well:

> Precisely because creation is the work of God's love, redemption is not something alien to the creator but rather something he will undertake with delight and glad self-giving . . . This is the plan that throughout the Bible is articulated in terms of God's choice of Israel as the means of redemption and then, after the long and checkered story of God and Israel, God's sending of his son, Jesus . . . What has happened in the death and resurrection of Jesus Christ, in other words, is by no means limited

---

11. Moltmann, *Theology of Hope*, 16.

12. Moltmann, *Theology of Hope*, 16.

13. Moltmann, *Theology of Hope*, 88.

14. Moltmann, *Theology of Hope*, 147.

to its effects on those human beings who believe the gospel and thereby find new life here and hereafter. It resonates out, in ways that we can't fully see or understand, into the vast recesses of the universe.[15]

When we speak about eschatology, we are not just talking about the events and various interpretations surrounding the *parousia*—the second coming of Jesus. Eschatology is not merely about the "end times" or "last things" as we, perhaps, have come to understand them. While the end times is one component, eschatology includes more than that. Eschatology points to where the future is going within the reliable and assured hope that God will fulfill all he has promised in Jesus Christ. In Jesus, God is saving and redeeming all creation from the effects of sin caused by human beings turning away from him. This future hope is assured because God has already fulfilled his promise in the resurrection of Jesus as Lord. God's future, therefore, is universal, or cosmic; it is at the same time already here (because Christ has come and is risen) and coming (because Christ will come again).[16] Eschatology, in this sense, points back to everything God has done and encompasses everything God has yet to do—yet we are assured will come to pass, because God has promised it. God is moving all creation toward his ultimate ends and repentance is how we align ourselves to the direction God is going.

Thus, for Christians, the story of the world is heading toward the fulfillment of the promises of God; that is the Christian hope. It is a hope assured because Christ has been raised. The resurrection proves God's righteousness, his faithfulness to his promises, and therefore the hope that all God has promised will come about.[17] This does not negate the importance of the end times, rather it puts them within their correct context.[18] The end times anticipate the ultimate consummation of God's rule, but a complete eschatology allows us to hope in that promise as we live under the lordship of Christ and live out the plan and purpose of God in the world, both today and tomorrow. Living in and living out God's ultimate ends makes the church the "Church for the world."[19] In the end, isn't that what we want the church to be? We want to be a church "engaged in the apostolate of hope

15. N.T. Wright, *Surprised by Hope*, 96–97.

16. See N. T. Wright, *Surprised by Hope*, 99; Witherington, *Jesus, Paul, and the End*, 20.

17. Moltmann, *Theology of Hope*, 204.

18. Wax so makes this point. He concludes, "Christians live today in light of the future, as people who trust in the promises of God and anticipate the return of Christ. Christian obedience, therefore, is grounded not merely in what God has done, but also in what God will do." Wax, "Eschatological Discipleship," 49–50.

19. Moltmann, *Theology of Hope*, 328.

for the world," a church propelled "like an arrow sent out into the world to point toward the future."[20]

Where does repentance fit into this kind of eschatological framework? We find our answer in the words of Peter. In 2 Peter 3, Peter addresses the second coming of Jesus, the *parousia*, within the context of God's larger promises, namely, the new heavens and the new earth (3:13).[21] Regarding this promise, Peter says God may seem slow to fulfill it. However, God is not slow; he is patient, and the reason for God's patience is repentance: "The Lord is not slow about His promise, as some count slowness, but is patient toward you, not wishing for any to perish but for all to come to repentance" (3:9). God's promises are coming; it is an assured hope, but before God will fulfill his promises and before God's ultimate future comes, he is allowing time for repentance. Repentance thus leads us into God's ultimate future. Not only that, but repentance, turning to God, is foundational to entering into the hope of God's promises.

Turning, returning, and realigning to God in Jesus, through the forgiveness of sins, and taking that message to the world is integral to our ultimate hope in God's ultimate future. In other words, if we want to move forward into God's future, it requires our turning. If we, as the church, can recapture this connection between repentance, mission, and eschatology, the message we will preach will be a message of hope and promise centered around three key components: the invitation to the kingdom of God, the transformation that comes by entering the kingdom, and the realization of a new reality that has come as a result of the kingdom. Jesus summarizes what his followers should pray for as praying for his kingdom to come and his will to be done (Matt 6:10). Jesus focuses the future on the kingdom and thus so should we.

THE FUTURE AND THE KINGDOM

To talk of God's future and where we are going, we must begin with the concept of kingdom.[22] We noted in chapter 3 that Jesus came announcing the kingdom of God, saying the kingdom is "at hand" (Matt 4:17 and Mark

20. Moltmann, *Theology of Hope*, 328.

21. Peter's intention is to focus his readers on the correct promise. He quotes the mockers first who ask, "Where is the promise of His coming" (2 Pet 3:3–4)? But he answers pointing toward God's bigger promise of the new creation—the new heavens and new earth, the realm of God's ultimate and complete rule, in the lordship of Jesus Christ. In Revelation 21, we find the unveiling of the new heavens and new earth in conjunction with God's presence and the inauguration of God's rule.

22. See Ladd, *Gospel of the Kingdom*, 14.

1:15).[23] Both John the Baptist and Jesus link the nearness of the kingdom with the coming of the Messiah—John preaching in anticipation of the coming of the Messiah and Jesus preaching as the Messiah who has come. Because Jesus has come, the kingdom has come as well.[24] While it has erupted into the world because Jesus has come, the kingdom is "an already *and* not-yet matter."[25] In Jesus it has come near; it is here and now, and yet it is still to come in its fullness when Jesus returns.

This means there are aspects of the kingdom available in the world today but some aspects must wait until the kingdom comes in its fullness at the return of Christ.[26] As Jesus uses the phrase, at times he refers to "God's present saving activity breaking into human history," while at other times he refers "to a future realm that one may enter as a result of that activity of God."[27] For example, Jesus can describe what the kingdom is like, yet he tells his disciples to pray for its coming (Matt 5:10). The kingdom can be seen in the ministry and miracles of Jesus, yet it is also the wedding feast for which one must be alert and ready to enter.[28] It is both here and yet to come.

How then do we experience the kingdom here? Both John the Baptist and Jesus link entering and experiencing the kingdom to repentance. Jesus often speaks of the kingdom being small, hidden, or contrary to the normal way the world seems to work and therefore is veiled. Many of those who hear Jesus "cannot see [the kingdom] because they face the wrong way . . . they must make a mental and spiritual U-turn, be converted, in order to believe (not see) that the good news is true: the reign of God is present."[29] Nevertheless, they are invited to enter into and experience the kingdom through repentance—by turning back to God.[30]

---

23. The Greek word in both texts is *eggizó* (*engikō*), which conveys the notion of being near, close, or immediate.

24. N. T. Wright says, "'God's kingdom' and 'kingdom of heaven' mean the same thing: the sovereign rule of God (that is, the rule of heaven, of the one who lives in heaven), which according to Jesus was and is breaking in to the present world, to earth." N. T. Wright, *Surprised by Hope*, 201.

25. Witherington, *Jesus, Paul and the End*, 52. Also see N. T. Wright, *Simply Jesus*, 117; N. T. Wright, *Jesus and the Victory*, 201; Moltmann, *Theology of Hope*, 217.

26. Witherington, *Jesus, Paul and the End*, 57.

27. Witherington, *Jesus, Paul and the End*, 59–60.

28. Also see Witherington, *Jesus, Paul and the End*, 66; and Ladd, *Gospel of the Kingdom*, 17–18.

29. Newbigin, *Gospel in a Pluralist Society*, 105. Again, I do not understand repentance as being synonymous with conversion, as Newbigin seems to indicate. However, as has been previously stated, they are two sides of the same coin.

30. See Ladd, *Gospel of the Kingdom*, 14.

What does this look like? We see other examples and applications through the rest of this chapter, but here we can begin by noting the Beatitudes show one of the most concrete pictures of how turning to God and discovering the kingdom in the small and hidden ways works in contrast to the way of the world (Matt 5:3–12; Luke 6:20–26.). We speak more about the Sermon on the Mount below. The Beatitudes help show us the way God makes himself known in the world. Jesus shows us that God works in ways (e.g., being poor, mourning, being gentle, being hungry, being persecuted) we often desire to turn away from. While most of our church communities may not be poor or persecuted or filled with those who are mourning or hungry, we are called to go to those who are and bring them into our congregations. An example of a church doing just that is discussed below.

We find this same invitation to enter into the kingdom through repentance within Peter's preaching in Acts. Peter does not directly preach about God's kingdom, but Peter definitely understands Jesus as being Lord, or King, and kingship implies a kingdom. In Acts 2:36, in Peter's conclusion to his Pentecost sermon, he says, "Therefore let all the house of Israel know for certain that God had made Him both Lord and Christ- this Jesus whom you crucified." We can unintentionally skip over the importance of this conclusion. By declaring Jesus to be Lord (King) and Christ (Messiah), Peter is pronouncing, "if Jesus was the Messiah, he was also the lord of the whole world."[31]

This pronouncement is what Old Testament passages (e.g., Psalms, Isaiah) said would happen.[32] In Acts 3:21, when Peter preaches about the "restoration of all things" as spoken by the prophets, he is referencing these and other Old Testament passages in which God rules as King and brings the restoration of his people. True kings reign over kingdoms, and a king without a kingdom holds little validity as a king. Jesus is King, and he is a true king. Jesus is King of a kingdom, the kingdom of God, which includes the physical world in which we live. As we said, aspects of that kingdom are on display now, while other aspects will only be realized when Jesus returns and the heavens and earth are remade. However, the response to the announcement of the kingdom and the invitation to come into the kingdom is the same for John the Baptist, Jesus, and Peter—repentance, turning to God and finding forgiveness for sins (Matt 3:2; 4:17; Acts 2:38; 3:19).

What we have often seen arising within the American evangelical church, however, is not a desire to move into the future of God's kingdom through repentance. Rather, we have seen a desire to essentially take control

31. N. T. Wright. *Resurrection of the Son*, 563.

32. See N. T. Wright, *Resurrection of the Son*, 564–66.

of our own future through the use of politics. This has given rise to Christian nationalism. Christian nationalism has been defined as "the belief that the American nation is defined by Christianity, and that the government should take active steps to keep it that way."[33] Similarly, Kristin Kobes Du Mez defines Christian nationalism as "the belief that America is God's chosen nation and must be defended as such."[34] Christian nationalism welds American and Christian ideals until they essentially become indistinguishable from one another and "advocates a fusion of Christianity with American civic life."[35] This kind of belief "takes Christian symbols, rhetoric, and concepts and weaves it into a political ideology that in its ideal form is idolatrous."[36] In the end, Christian nationalism "takes the name of Christ for a worldly political agenda, proclaiming that its program is *the* political program for every true believer . . . it is taking the name of Christ as a fig leaf to cover its political program, treating the message of Jesus as a tool of political propaganda and the church as the handmaiden and cheerleader of the state."[37]

The problem with Christian nationalism, or any form of idolatry, whether it comes from religious conservatives or progressives, from the political left or right, is the ideology becomes coequal with God. The ideology becomes an object of worship and ends up taking the place of God as the means through which God works in the world and establishes his kingdom. Instead of God working through his followers and his church, God must work through whatever political ideology, economic system, or social cause we have made equal to God. Some of these causes may even be good and just; however, if we make them equal to God, they have become idols. God desires to be the only one we worship. God must be the one we love with all our heart, soul, and mind, and there are no other gods we can put before him (Matt 22:37 and Exod 20:3)—including political, social, and religious ideologies by any name.

While Christian nationalism remains a minority movement within the United States, those who hold to Christian nationalist views tend to be more dogmatic. In fact, researchers concluded that "Christian nationalism is the leading predictor that white Americans are more dogmatic," which they define as being "unwilling to consider the possibility that they could be wrong, that they are unwilling to change their views even in the face of conflicting

33. P. D. Miller, "What Is Christian Nationalism?," paragraph 5.

34. Du Mez, *Jesus and John Wayne*, 4.

35. M. Lee, "Christian Nationalism is Worse," paragraph 7.

36. M. Lee, "Christian Nationalism is Worse," paragraph 10.

37. P. D. Miller, "What Is Christian Nationalism?," paragraph 12. Emphasis original.

evidence."[38] Christian nationalism has also been found to be linked to the affirmation of "baseless conspiracies, including QAnon myths, antisemitic tropes, rampant voter fraud, Trump's 'Big Lie' and general [COVID-19] vaccine misinformation."[39]

One telling example of this idolatry took place during the Christmas season in 2021 at First Baptist Church in Dallas, Texas. On this particular Sunday, the special guest was former president Donald Trump, whose face was featured on the cover of the worship bulletin that Sunday.[40] Throughout the sermon that morning, pastor Robert Jeffress made mention of Trump and highlighted their friendship.[41] The pinnacle of the service came when Trump addressed the congregation, walking to the stage to the sound of a standing ovation.[42] Trump used the opportunity to speak on the "'great trouble' facing America" while mentioning "border security, inflation, gas prices and the U.S. withdrawal from Afghanistan."[43] Within the same remarks Trump conceded, "Our country needs a savior right now, and we have a savior—that's not me, that's someone much higher," and that "the life and death and resurrection of Jesus Christ forever changed the world."[44] Trump continued:

> It's impossible to think of the life of our own country without the influence of his example and of his teachings; our miraculous founding, overcoming civil war, abolishing slavery, defeating communism and fascism, reaching boundless heights of science and discovering so many incredible things . . . and the United States ultimately becoming a truly great nation—and we're going to keep it that way, keep it that way, not going to let it go, we're not going to let it go—but none of those could have ever happened without Jesus Christ and his followers and his church.[45]

This mixing of politics and religion defines Christian nationalism. The blend of political language and ideology with religious language and ideology make the two almost indistinguishable from each other. What is constant, however, is the hope of forming the kingdom through the will and

38. Perry, "Dogmatism of Christian Nationalism," subtitle, paragraph 14.

39. Perry, "Dogmatism of Christian Nationalism," paragraph 4.

40. Lupfer, "At First Baptist Dallas," paragraph 6.

41. Black, "Even Bob Dylan Knows," paragraphs 12, 15–17.

42. First Baptist Dallas, "Christmas Greeting from Donald J. Trump," 2:00–2:44.

43. Prosser, "5 Takeaways," paragraphs 6, 8.

44. First Baptist Dallas, "Christmas Greeting from Donald J. Trump," 7:50–8:15.

45. First Baptist Dallas, "Christmas Greeting from Donald J. Trump," 8:16–9:17.

actions of a certain political lens. This is absolutely contradictory to the way Jesus said his kingdom would come and how he said his kingdom would be seen in the world.[46] Most of all, Christian nationalism preaches that entry into the kingdom, which has become synonymous with America, comes through political advancement and legal protections that come from a "Christian nation,"[47] not through repentance and turning/returning to God.

Living as agents of repentance within God's mission entails living under the lordship of Jesus, as his church, and includes following Jesus' ways and turning toward him and finding liberation as we turn away from sin and live in the reality of Jesus' lordship. Within this community of the kingdom, we are able to experience the turning in allegiance to God that Paul describes in Acts 26:18 and Colossians 1:13–14. It is through repentance that Jesus invites us to enter into his kingdom here and now through repentance.

We live in a world where so many entities vie for our allegiance and so many forces seek to reign and rule over our lives. In contrast, the mission of the church, in common with what we saw in the preaching of Peter and Paul, is to announce that the world's true King has come. Unlike the other entities and forces that vie for our allegiance, the kingdom of God proclaimed by Jesus is a kingdom in which we find freedom. This freedom isn't found as we turn away from God and live free from him; rather it's a liberation, as Moltmann says, that comes as we turn to him and turn away from the sin that truly enslaves us, and enter into the kingdom of God.

Within Matthew's gospel, Jesus' fullest explanation and description of the kingdom of God comes within the Sermon on the Mount. In a recent dissertation, Moses Kintu argues the Sermon on the Mount "should be understood as the first detailed description of the message summarized in Matt 4:17."[48] I agree with this overall assessment. When kingdom and repentance are linked, we discover the entire Sermon on the Mount stands as a sermon on repentance. Every place Jesus contrasts the old with the new, and every place Jesus calls his followers to live in a new way, he is calling his followers to embrace repentance. The sermon is also eschatological, as it anticipates the way the world will be as it is redeemed. Thus, it also is missional. The sermon is one of the clearest descriptions of how God's kingdom stands in contrast to the kingdoms of the world, which attempt to garner our allegiance and subject us under their rule. To individuals and communities who are under such kingdoms, the hope and promise of God's kingdom stands as liberation and freedom made possible by turning or returning to God.

46. See Matt 13, for example.

47. See M. Lee, "Christian Nationalism."

48. Kintu, "Repentance in the Sermon," 2.

Additionally, Paul tells us the kingdom of God is "righteousness and peace and joy in the Holy Spirit" (Rom 14:17). As attributes of the kingdom, they are attributes originating from God. And as we were created to desire God, these are attributes we naturally desire. Beyond that these are characteristics that the entities of the world—like government and politics, materialism, and even religion and philosophy—promise. Uncoupled from God and from their participation in the kingdom, each one promises to make the world right, to bring peace, and to bring happiness, yet all their promises are empty. At the same time, attempting to inaugurate the kingdom through any of these other means leads to a bastardization and co-opting of the message of the kingdom. Jesus makes clear the way of the kingdom is the way of repentance, of turning, returning, and realigning with God through Jesus himself. Only within the kingdom of God can we experience righteousness, peace, and joy, and each of these comes as we turn or turn back to God in repentance.

THE FUTURE AND TRANSFORMATION

In the same way that we have many entities vying for our allegiance, so many things attempt to sell us on transformation, or at least the appearance of outward transformation, regardless of whether any actual inward change has taken place. We'll be transformed, they tell us, when we buy the latest model of car or the newest technology. We'll be transformed when we dress a certain way, when our body looks a certain way, or when we attain a certain amount of wealth or status. Our whole advertising industry is built on the promise of transformation. By offering the promise of transformation, the advertising industry realizes the desire of human beings to be changed from what they are to something else. However, whereas our products are limited to mainly external transformation, God desires to transform us, our communities, our world, and our churches from the inside out.

Entering into the kingdom of God brings transformation.[49] As we already mentioned above, as Jesus teaches on the characteristics of the kingdom, he constantly emphasizes the ways in which the kingdom of God turns upside down and transforms the world as it is. Beyond transforming the world as it is, the kingdom also transforms people as they are. Thus,

---

49. Ladd writes, "The Gospel must not only offer a personal salvation in the future life to those who believe; it must also transform all of the relationships of life here and now and thus cause the Kingdom of God to prevail in all the world." Ladd, *Gospel of the Kingdom*, 15.

transformation is cosmological, individual, and corporate. All three are aspects of God's ultimate ends.

Jesus manifests individual transformation by healing the sick, exorcising demons, raising the dead, and even more importantly by forgiving sins. The transformation we see Jesus bringing is a prologue to the transformation we see coming in Revelation 21:4–5. On Pentecost we find a whole community transformed as the Holy Spirit descends and empowers the church. Additionally, part of the mission given to the disciples, and to us, in Jesus' commission recorded in Mark 16:15–16 is announcing transformation has come through Jesus. The signs recorded in Mark indicate the mission of the disciples is to be a continuation of Jesus' ministry. The signs also echo scriptures like Isaiah 11:6–9, which describe the transformation coming as a result of the Messiah.

As we enter the kingdom and advance toward the future to which God is moving all creation, a central piece of the transformation coming as a result of repentance is the chance to see the world in the way God sees it. We introduced this idea in chapter 4 when we defined repentance. Not only is transformation an aspect of repentance as we respond to God; to be agents of repentance as we continue the *missio Dei* in the world necessitates a transformation in the way we see the world. In particular, it requires a transformation in the way we view human beings, as men and women created in the image of God, as we mentioned in chapter 2. As the church seeks to fulfill its mission within God's eschatological future, we must be a church committed to living out the kind of transformation we find occurring through repentance.

Throughout his letters, the apostle Paul emphasizes the transformational aspect of the gospel—often using himself as the prime example. As a Pharisee, zealous for the law, Paul had believed he was aligned with God and God's purposes. But when Paul saw Jesus, put his faith in him as Lord and Christ, and turned toward and truly realigned himself with God, he was transformed. He describes it as a new life (Rom 6:4), a new self (Eph 4:24; Col 3:10), and a new creature (2 Cor 5:17; Gal 6:15). This transformed life is the result of the message of the gospel and of the repentance Paul says he is faithful to preach to Jew and Gentile alike. In Jesus the divide between Jew and Gentile had been torn down (Eph 2:14) and Paul's message is that everyone, Jew and Gentile, should repent and turn to God (Acts 26:20). Not only has the divide been broken down between Jew and Gentile, but also between male and female and slave and free (Gal 3:28). Thus, all people, regardless of race, ethnicity, sex, or socioeconomic class, are able to turn to God and enter into the kingdom. This, again, is a preview of God's future as we find in Revelation 7:9.

In short, Paul's turning to God transformed the way he viewed people. We cannot neglect this part of Paul's gospel transformation. Once he encountered Jesus and understood the eschatological and cosmic significance of Jesus' death, resurrection, and ascension as King, he came to understand this message is for all people, again as he makes clear in Acts 26:20. Under this transformational understanding, Paul is thus able to describe the community of the church as a singular body (Rom 12; 1 Cor 12). When we turn to God, we enter into a single kingdom and become members of a single body. However, what all too often marks the American evangelical church today is division, and a walling off between the church and those the church is on a mission to reach.

Whether the issue is immigration, race relations, or addressing poverty—among other issues—the place we must begin is with a transformed view of men and women as being created in the image of God. On our own accord, we are hesitant, wary, and threatened by those we do not know. This leads to fear, and fear—all too often—leads to violence. Within the church, these same forces lead to indifference and thus disengagement. As one writer provocatively states,

> Churches that are unprepared for the leadership challenges presented by rapid population growth, or unwilling to become involved in the social needs of new arrivals, or unaware of how to help their middle-class congregants leverage their privileges for the well-being of these new arms and legs in the body of Christ will become irrelevant, mere socio-economic enclaves, and ignored by a new humanity set in motion.[50]

If, however, we are truly repentant people and have turned and realigned ourselves with God and desire to engage in and continue God's mission in the world, we cannot neglect men and women made in God's image, thus making our churches become irrelevant and ignored. In many of our church communities, the irrelevant and ignored include those who are unlike us in color, language, or culture.

One recent study found white evangelicals (35 percent) were the least likely group to agree that "the growing number of newcomers from other countries strengthens American society."[51] In contrast, the religiously unaffiliated are the most likely (at 74 percent) to agree with the same statement.[52] Another startling contrast exists between white evangelicals and Black Protestants. Whereas only 35 percent of white evangelicals agreed with the above

---

50. White, "Waves of Blessing," 75.

51. Jenkins, "Immigration Reform," paragraph 11.

52. Jenkins, "Immigration Reform," paragraph 12.

statement, 69 percent of Black Protestants agree.[53] Obviously, something is amiss in the way a majority of white evangelicals view those from other cultures. It seems they have decided they cannot share their country now with those they may very well share eternity with in the kingdom. The fear of people from different cultures leads to disengagement with the gospel, as well as a failure to see such people as valuable to God, yet that's exactly how God sees them—as human beings who are valuable and who need to turn to him.

To see people from God's perspective entails seeing all people as returning to God, in the same way we have returned to God. Being agents of repentance within God's mission and toward God's future requires us to engage our world in the way God did and in the way Jesus did, and to center our proclamation of the gospel on the God who turned toward us in Jesus. We cannot build back the walls Jesus tore down. We must go to those unlike us because they are like God. This kind of inside-out transformation occurs in our hearts when we turn/return to God and realign ourselves to see the world in the way God sees the world.

Eastbrook Church in Milwaukee, Wisconsin, is one local church that seems to be engaging its community in this way. The church engages in ministries to international college students and runs the International Community Center in an area of the city many immigrants and refugees now call home.[54] Dan Ryan, senior director of mission, says the church's mission to engage immigrants and refugees comes from the way "these folks are treasured by God and valuable in his sight."[55] Eastbrook Church appears to be an example of what turning to God is—being transformed to see people in the way God does, and engaging in God's mission because the dividing walls have been torn down.

The question is: what keeps more of our churches from engaging those around us in such a transformational way? The answer must begin with a lack of repentance, by which I mean a lack of aligning with God and, as a result, not being transformed to see the world in the way that God sees it. Our world is anxious to see a Christianity that produces a radical change of life. Repentance and realigning ourselves with God and with his mission and purposes is the way to this transformed life. Thus, as the church we cannot be shy in proclaiming repentance as a necessary response to the message of the gospel. We must follow the examples of Peter and Paul and

---

53. Jenkins, "Immigration Reform," paragraph 12.

54. Smietana, "At Milwaukee Church," paragraph 5.

55. Smietana, "At Milwaukee Church," paragraph 21.

preach repentance. By doing so, we are allowed to live in an advancement of God's ultimate ends.

I challenge every pastor, church leader, and church to live out this kind of repentance by taking a seemingly radical step. Within your unique context, identify the people group the most *unlike* the current makeup of your church congregation. This people group may be different because of their race, ethnicity, sex, socioeconomic status, political beliefs, or lifestyle choices. Then begin praying for this people group as men and women created in the image of God. Also pray the church would be realigned with God and be transformed—this is repentance. Finally, after realigning in prayer and seeking transformation, even if it takes months as this may be a slow process, then seek ways to connect with this group while ministering to their needs and engaging them with the message of the gospel.

A NEW REALITY

As the people of God, the church represents a new reality that has dawned in the lordship of Jesus Christ. As a result of the inauguration of the kingdom and the transformation available as we turn and realign with God and his mission and see the world, especially people, in the way God sees the world, we live in a new reality that exists in contrast to, while being in the midst of, the present fallen reality. In this sense the church is an eschatological preview for the world. Whereas the world and its people in our present reality are marked by division, within the people of God, "there is neither Jew nor Greek, there is neither slave nor free man, there is neither male nor female" (Gal 3:28). Whereas the current reality is subjected to death and the dominion of darkness (Rom 5:17; Col 1:13), the people of God have been made alive and made to shine "as lights in the world" (Phil 2:15).

The eschatological reality of which we are a part is a reality where the old things have passed away and new things have come (2 Cor 5:17). We gain a clearer understanding of the change between the old and new in Galatians 5:16–24. Repentance and turning to God in Jesus comes between the old and the new. Living in realization of the new reality that exists in Jesus and unveiling that reality to a lost world must be part of the church's mission in the world. Proclaiming repentance in Jesus' name (Luke 24:47) and declaring that the world has been and is in the process of being transformed (Mark 16:17–18) mean a new reality has indeed come; a reality where men and women are connected to God and connected to one another. Within this new reality, we discover repentance and turning/returning to God involves a movement toward justice as a mark of the kingdom.

In chapter 3, we noted Jesus' teachings in Matthew 11, where he offers the removal of one yoke and the taking up of the yoke of the Messiah. This transfer of yokes helps to mark the people of God. We noted the connection between Matthew 11 and Isaiah 58. In Isaiah 58, the yoke is the yoke of injustice that must be broken.[56] The connection between Isaiah 58 and Matthew 11 seems to imply the cities of Chorazin, Bethsaida, and Capernaum need to turn from injustices, which also describes Tyre, Sidon, and Sodom.[57] This also connects back to Jesus' words in response to the messengers from John at the beginning of Matthew 11. Jesus answers the question of whether he is the Messiah by citing his miracles (Matt 11:4–6). These miracles are miracles of justice as much as they are miracles of healing. Interestingly, Jesus does not mention release of the captives, as John is in prison. Perhaps this is an indication that, even though Jesus is here, some injustices aren't going to be remedied until a time in the future. We do, however, get a glimpse of this future in Revelation 21:4, where we find the effects of injustice—tears, death, mourning, crying, and pain—have passed away as a result of the full unveiling of the kingdom at the time of the *parousia*.

The opportunity for repentance Jesus condemns the cities for rejecting is the same offer Jesus gives to us. We do not want to follow in their rejection of God's justice. As God's people in the new reality, the new kingdom Jesus has inaugurated, we also must turn to God to live as agents of repentance and justice. There are almost too many specific injustices we could cite at this point. A few include instances of discrimination and exploitation (sexual, racial, religious, economic), narcissism (especially within church leadership[58]), patriarchism, and an all-too-prevalent vindictive and judgmental attitude. Such injustice requires an individualized effort to address the injustice and make a turn to God and a turn toward justice. Is there something, then, connecting each of these? Is there an application we find applying across situations?

Justin Giboney, president of the AND Campaign, which seeks to "educate and organize Christians for civil and cultural engagement" and

---

56. See Grogan, *Isaiah*, 325.

57. Jesus cites as parallels Tyre, Sidon, and Sodom. From Ezekiel 26–27 and Isaiah 23, it appears Tyre and Sidon's wealth led them to exalt themselves above the place of God, as well as engage in unjust trade practices. Additionally, Ezekiel 16:49–50 records, "Behold, this was the guilt of your sister Sodom: she and her daughters had arrogance, abundant food and careless ease, but she did not help the poor and needy. Thus they were haughty and committed abominations before Me. Therefore I removed them when I saw it."

58. See DeGroat, *When Narcissism Comes to Church*.

participate in "redemptive justice,"[59] argues Christian justice must begin with an acknowledgement of sin—and compassion.[60] Giboney notes some non-Christian, as well as Christian, justice advocates have "rightly responded to a culture that ignores systemic sins. But they've done so by ignoring *individual* [sic] sin."[61] He continues,

> We live in a culture that's losing the ethic and the will to discourage mentalities that lead to sex work, recreational drug use, and family abandonment. We'd rather find ways to excuse them than stand on unpopular principles. But gospel-driven compassion doesn't conceptually refashion or normalize our brokenness in vain attempts to evade categories of sin. True justice isn't inclusive of sin, because sin leads to moral disorder, and moral disorder is where injustice thrives.[62]

What Giboney advocates is an understanding of broader social injustices tied to individual sin. A culture, society, or church can only sin as its individual members participate in sin—either actively or passively. Thus, the connection point to addressing areas of injustice is the addressing of sin, including the individual sin that leads to societal sin. This is one of the "unpopular principles" Giboney mentions above. We talk more in the final chapter about how we can address our individual sinfulness.

The issue for now is: how does repentance enable us to address sin in a compassionate way? Anyone can stand on the street corner and pronounce judgment on certain sins. However, just like the Pharisees and the woman caught in adultery in John 8, decrying sin without compassion can easily lead to its own form of injustice, such as the vindictive and judgmental attitude mentioned above. Rather, Jesus responds with truthfulness and compassion. While the word "repent" is not found in the narrative, the theme certainly is. Jesus calls her to a new way of life, and to "go" from her way of sin and leave it behind. This certainly looks like the act of repentance in action. In Jesus we see the way we address sin in a compassionate way is through repentance. Repentance is a grace and the opportunity to turn/return to God in repentance is a wonderful example of God's compassionate love toward us. Thus, the justice toward which God is moving creation is found through the act of repentance. As the church, we must begin to see that God's mission of repentance and justice are deeply connected and therefore one cannot occur without the other, and both move us toward God's ultimate future.

59. AND Campaign, "About," paragraph 2.
60. Giboney, "Christian Virtue Strengthens," paragraph 4.
61. Giboney, "Christian Virtue Strengthens," paragraph 13
62. Giboney, "Christian Virtue Strengthens," paragraph 16.

CONCLUSION

In Jesus the kingdom has come, the world has been and now is transformed, and a new reality has come. In him a new world has been born, a world God is moving toward his ultimate ends. As God's people, we've been tasked to continue God's mission in the world, and we do this, partly, as agents of repentance. Throughout this chapter, we have explored where God's story ultimately is going and have seen three ways we can be engaged as God moves creation toward his ultimate ends. In each case, repentance plays an important part. Repentance is our means of entering the kingdom of God, it is the way we are transformed to begin to see the world in the way God sees the world, and it is the way that we live in the new reality of justice that Jesus initiated and is in the process of completing. Let's turn now to our final chapter, where we examine three characteristics our churches, and the individuals who make up our churches, will have if we are truly aligned with God and actively pursuing God's mission in the world.

7

Living the Repentance Mission

As CERTAIN PARTS OF the United States began emerging from the shadow of COVID-19, Mike Cosper, in his podcast *The Rise and Fall of Mars Hill*, helped to cast a spotlight onto the shadows remaining following the resignation of Mark Driscoll from Mars Hill Church. Trevin Wax provides a helpful and concise summary of the narrative covered in the podcast:

> The show follows the story of Mars Hill Church, founded in Seattle in 1996 by Mark Driscoll. The episodes chronicle the rise of Driscoll and his church's influence within conservative evangelicalism, describing patterns of unhealthy leadership that resulted in the diminishment of Driscoll's credibility and the dissolution of the church (in its original form).[1]

Cosper's popular podcast provides many worthy points of discussion for churches, church leaders, and church members on the topics of leadership, conflict resolution, and authority. Portions of the podcast are also helpful for our discussion throughout the upcoming pages. At the outset we must acknowledge it is not only megachurches or celebrity pastors who are susceptible to the issues, temptations, and sin uncovered in Cosper's reporting. The same issues can infect church leaders and churches of any size. Nevertheless, Mars Hill and Driscoll himself provide crucial examples of the necessity of developing the characteristics needed to carry out and live out the repentance mission. The reason for this is because even more than

---

1. Wax, "On 'Mars Hill,'" paragraph 1.

the actions of Driscoll and Mars Hill, it was the attitudes underlying those actions that were the real cause of their downfall.

The Mars Hill story began as a testimony to church-planting success. As one of the least Christian cities in the United States, Seattle seemed like an unlikely place for a megachurch to form. However, Driscoll and Mars Hill were able to reach thousands of men and women in the Seattle area with the life-changing message of the gospel. Those in Seattle were just the beginning of Driscoll's growing reach and fame. As an early adopter of podcasting, Driscoll was able to have millions of people hear his, often brash, preaching. His broad reach, what we would today call his "platform," made Driscoll a celebrity, especially within the "young, restless, and Reformed" circle he affiliated with at the time. The source of Driscoll's fame, however, also ended up becoming the source of the downfall of both Driscoll and Mars Hill. This is the story Cosper tells within his podcast.

Throughout the podcast, Cosper and those he interviews identify an attitude of pride, unforgiveness, and vindictiveness that became, like a crumbling foundation, the ultimate cause of the church's and Driscoll's collapse.[2] These attitudes can be found within church leaders, and even church members, regardless of the size of a church. The characteristics mentioned above make it hard, if not impossible, for the church to join in the *missio Dei* and preach the message that men and women everywhere need to turn to God. What characteristics, then, do our churches need to develop?

What does it look like to engage in God's mission in the world, the *missio Dei*, as agents of repentance? In the previous chapter our focus was on where the ultimate end of the mission of repentance leads us. We saw how repentance moves us, as the people of God, into God's ultimate future. As we complete our study, our focus in this chapter is to gaze on what we as the church can become if we embody repentance as we have been exploring it.

Here is where we bring discipleship and spiritual formation into our conversation. Mission and discipleship are inescapably linked, as we see in Jesus' words in Matthew 28:19–20. Discipleship, most basically, is the process of becoming more like Jesus as we live our lives following him. As Jim Putman and Bobby Harrington put it in their book *Discipleshift*, "The ideal life is focused on Jesus. It is not just trusting him but also truly following

---

2. These are not the only issues Cosper raises in regard to Mark Driscoll and Mars Hill. Other problems identified include toxic masculinity, spiritual abuse, poisonous church culture, as well as lack of the character and integrity needed to be exhibited by a pastor. It is beyond the purpose of this chapter to delve deeply into each of these issues. This chapter is not a point-by-point critique of Mars Hill and Mark Driscoll; rather Mars Hill and Driscoll serve as symptomatic examples of deeper underlying needs that I seek to address.

him . . . It is about becoming more and more like him in the power of the Holy Spirit to the glory of God."[3] One of the ways we become more like Jesus is as we engage in the *missio Dei*, a major component of which is repentance, as we have explored. We want to see how repentance fits into discipleship and spiritual formation, and forms us into the people and into the church on mission in the world.

In this chapter we find, in contrast to the pride, unforgiveness, and vindictiveness that characterized Mars Hill, humility brings us to repentance and makes us forgiving, repentance is an act of love that makes us loving, and, finally, repentance as part of spiritual formation makes us disciple-making. In these ways we live the mission of repentance and can see our whole lives, and our mission in the world, as one of turning—as Martin Luther said. As we turn our attention to the relationship between repentance and discipleship, our discussion includes new conversation partners from throughout the long history and various traditions of Christianity. The small number of theologians cited in this chapter are by no means the only voices that could be included in the conversation.

TURNING DOWN: HUMILITY

The Catholic theologian and Trappist monk Thomas Merton says, "Humility consists in being precisely the person you actually are before God."[4] He goes on to say, "It is almost impossible to overestimate the value of true humility and its power in the spiritual life."[5] For Merton the power of humility rests in its ability to move us out of self-centeredness, and self-centeredness and pride go hand in hand. However, humility allows us to come before God and acknowledge we are men and women who have turned from him and turned to worship ourselves—or any number of other idols. Humility allows us to turn down our pride and see ourselves for who we truly are—sinners in desperate need of God. We have discussed sin before in this work; however, here we add another layer to our understanding of sin and repentance as it relates to spiritual formation and discipleship. Then we close this section by exploring how humility leads us to live as agents of repentance through forgiveness.

As human beings, we have a tendency to hide our sinfulness from ourselves and in doing so we deceive ourselves. Our pride moves us to minimize the wrongs we do and see ourselves in the best light. A recent study

3. Putman and Harrington, *Discipleshift*, 31.

4. Merton, *New Seeds of Contemplation*, 99.

5. Merton, *New Seeds of Contemplation*, 181.

found 65 percent of American adults agreed with the statement, "Everyone sins a little, but most people are good by nature."[6] This points to a general attitude of elevating ourselves to the category of "good," and while we can point to a few bad apples, we almost certainly don't see ourselves in such a category. Thus, we fail to see ourselves as sinners and, at the same time, fail to see the seriousness of the sin we do see in ourselves. John speaks directly to this: "If we say that we have no sin, we are deceiving ourselves and the truth is not in us" (1 John 1:8).

No one desires to see himself or herself as a sinner. Most people, as we've seen above, tend to have an optimistic view of their own morality. However, there are those who find themselves trapped in despair and self-loathing because of their mistakes and therefore cannot see themselves as objects of God's love, mercy, and forgiveness. God desires for us to see our sin so we can turn to him for salvation, as Paul writes in 1 Timothy 1:15, "Christ Jesus came into the world to save sinners." Many of us, though, even if we feel brokenness, emptiness, and shame inside of ourselves, try to pass the responsibility or blame for our sin onto others.[7] The humility to see ourselves as the sinners we are and take responsibility for our own wrongs is the beginning point of repentance. Humility moves us into the position to return to God, find forgiveness, and participate in God's mission in the world. A certain level of humility is prerequisite to repentance.

Before looking at reasons why we flee from humility and therefore flee from repentance, let's define biblical humility. Without trying to develop a full biblical theology of humility, we clearly see two defining aspects of humility within Scripture. Beginning with the words of Jesus, we see humility stands as the opposite to self-exaltation and pride. Jesus says, "Whoever exalts himself shall be humbled; and whoever humbles himself shall be exalted" (Matt 23:12). We find similar statements in Luke 1:52; 14:11; 18:14; James 4:10; and 1 Peter 5:6. All of these scriptures set self-exaltation and humility as opposites. God brings down the former and lifts up the latter. We might say, although perhaps somewhat crudely, the Bible tells us to turn ourselves down so God can turn us up.[8]

Pride is set alongside self-exaltation. Not only does God humble the exalted; God opposes the proud but gives grace to the humble (Jas 4:6).

---

6. Lifeway Research, "American Theology Study 2020," 14.

7. I think immediately of Adam and Eve in the garden of Eden in Genesis 3. Eve blamed the serpent for his deception. Adam blamed God for Eve's existence and therefore her ability to sin. Adam also blamed Eve for giving the fruit to him. I imagine if God asked the serpent, the serpent would have blamed God for making him crafty.

8. This turning down is not a turning to self-loathing, but rather to a humility to see ourselves as we really are—not better than we are or worse than we are.

James continues by linking pride to the need to turn from sin and turn to God (Jas 4:7–10). While James does not use the word "repent," he is definitely speaking to the theme. Pride and self-exaltation therefore stand as opposites to humility and stand in the way of turning to God. David Brooks, in his book *The Second Mountain*, outlines the many forms pride can take. He mentions pride in oneself, intellectual pride, moral pride, and even religious pride.[9] In Matthew 23 Jesus critiques the scribes and Pharisees for their pride and self-exaltation. Instead of leading with humility and as servants to the people, these religious leaders are guilty of tying heavy burdens on others while demanding those same people lift them up as they lift up themselves.

Self-exaltation and pride show themselves in the worshiping of ourselves or some projection of ourselves above God, which the Bible calls idolatry. In pride we set ourselves above all others, including God, as the object of our worship. In idolatry we set created things above God, the creator (Rom 1:25). Pride is also seen when we refuse to take responsibility, and thus we set ourselves above God as the ones who are able to declare what is right or wrong. God, however, does not share glory and Scripture promises all things will be subjected to God and every knee will bow before Jesus Christ—the one God has exalted above all things (Isa 42:8; 1 Cor 15:28; Phil 2:10). All things, including human beings, will be humbled before God. Before that time, however, God invites us to humility.

Throughout the Mars Hill Church story, one of the consistent themes was the pride of Mark Driscoll. Mars Hill Church was, as Driscoll told the story, his vision and its rise and success were due to him and his leadership and preaching. Driscoll set himself up as the example. Cosper, in the episode "Aftermath," says one of Driscoll's core messages, as he quotes one former Mars Hill member, was, "You suck; do better; do like me."[10] This pride, or arrogance, was cited by the Mars Hill elders within their investigation of Driscoll after his resignation.[11]

Pride, arrogance, and self-exaltation are not vices only for megachurch pastors. Merton reminds us we are all susceptible to pride; he calls pride the "worm in the hearts of all religious men."[12]

While Paul does tell the Corinthians to imitate him (1 Cor 11:1), he sets this within an important context. First, he tells them to imitate him "just as" he imitates Christ. Paul is not telling the Corinthians to imitate him

9. Brooks, *Second Mountain*, 239–40.

10. Cosper, "Aftermath," 42:04.

11. Shellnutt, "Mark Driscoll Is Still 'Unrepentant,'" paragraph 7.

12. Merton, *New Seeds of Contemplation*, 48–49.

because he has everything figured out. Rather, his call is to imitate him in just the same way he is imitating Jesus Christ. Second, this saying comes as the conclusion of Paul's admonition in 10:31–33. His point in these verses is to explain the reason why he does everything he does as an apostle and preacher is to give glory to God while not seeking his own profit but the profit of others so they may be saved. Paul calls the Corinthians to imitate him in this way, not in the prideful way Driscoll called his church to follow him. Paul's call is actually a call of humility, rather than pride. What we find throughout Scripture is humility stands in contrast to pride.

If humility stands in contrast to pride and self-exaltation, how then can we define humility?[13] Within the Old Testament, two components of humility are seen in a variety of Scriptures. First, we see humility is a position, a posture, before God. Second, we see one can humble oneself or one can be humbled by God. "Humble before the Lord" is a common phrase found in the Old Testament. To note just two examples, in Exodus 10:3, Moses and Aaron ask Pharaoh on God's behalf, "How long will you refuse to humble yourself before Me?" Additionally, in 2 Chronicles 34:27, God commends Josiah "because [his] heart was tender and [he] humbled himself before Me." Humility begins as a position before God. The Hebrew word *'ānāh* pictures being bowed down or bended, connoting a posture.[14] Thus, humility is a heart position in which one comes before God and bows himself or herself before him. Humility includes a posture of vulnerability and a position of accepting whatever God desires to do. According to the passages we have examined, we know what God desires. God desires to lift up and exalt the humble. Psalm 113:7–9 says, "He raises the poor from the dust and lifts the needy from the ash heap, to make them sit with princes, with the princes of his people. He makes the barren woman abide in the house as a joyful mother of children. Praise the Lord!"

Through the Old Testament we also see humility as a posture we can choose. However, we also see either we can humble ourselves or God will humble us. The only way to approach God is through humility. In grace, God gives us the opportunity to humble ourselves. If we do not humble ourselves, however, God will humble us—as we see in Deuteronomy 8, for example. In that passage God humbles his people to discipline them, teach them, and bring them to obedience in keeping his commands. Jesus describes himself as humble (Matt 11:29). The apostle Paul tells us Jesus humbled himself by becoming obedient to the Father (Phil 2:8). Jesus chose

13. Roberts says, "The contrasting subjects of pride and humility are among the most prominent themes in the Bible." Roberts, *Repentance*, 185.

14. Koehler and Baumgartner, *Hebrew and Aramaic Lexicon*, 484–85.

the posture of humility. Dane Ortlund writes that Jesus' humility, or the character of being lowly, points to Jesus' accessibility. "For all his resplendent glory and dazzling holiness, his supreme uniqueness and otherness, no one in human history has ever been more approachable than Jesus Christ," he writes.[15] While accessibility is a component of Jesus' humility, Jesus' choosing of humility stands as our ultimate example. Jesus, who was equal to God, did not hold on to equality but chose humility in order to become obedient to the will of the Father (Phil 2:6–8).

How then can we define biblical or Christian humility? I propose we can define it as *a chosen posture before God in which we become accepting and obedient to God's discipline, teaching, and will.* In humility we turn down the exaltation of ourselves and the pride that causes us to put ourselves above others and above God. As mentioned above, humility is an aspect of repentance. In fact, humility is the beginning point of repentance. Humility moves us into the position to return to God and find forgiveness. Henri Nouwen speaks to this, saying,

> One of the greatest challenges of the spiritual life is to receive God's forgiveness. There is something in us humans that keeps us clinging to our sin and prevents us from letting God erase our past and offer us a completely new beginning. Sometimes it even seems as though I want to prove to God that my darkness is too great to overcome . . . Receiving forgiveness requires a total willingness to let God be God and do all the healing, restoring, and renewing. As long as I want to do even a part of that myself, I end up with partial solutions.[16]

This letting "God be God" echoes Merton. When God is God and we come to him exactly as we are, we must come as repentant people—humbled, without self-exaltation or pride, and accepting and obedient to God's discipline, teaching, and will. In short, we become the people we were created to be. In addition to that, we become more like Jesus. In Matthew 11:29, Jesus describes himself as humble in heart.

What then might make us flee from humility and seek to exalt ourselves and live a life of pride that places ourselves above others and above God? We could point to many possible motives; however, Augustine defines one that surely lies at the root of all the others. Within *Confessions*, Augustine repeatedly speaks to the theme of desire. We fail to acknowledge God and we fail to come to God in humility because we would rather pursue our own desires. Early within the book Augustine prays, "Grant this, so that

15. Ortlund, *Gentle and Lowly*, 20.

16. Nouwen, *Prodigal Son*, 53.

you may grow sweet to me about all the allurements that I followed after . . . For when I learned vain things, you gave instruction to me. You forgave me my sin of delight in those vanities."[17] Here Augustine acknowledges sin is an allurement because it appears sweet and delightful and thus awakens our desires. These desires in and of themselves are not bad—as God gives us desires; sin, however, entices us to fulfill those desires in ways that go against God's design.[18] Augustine acknowledges this as well. Later, he talks of sin as the fulfilling of desires that belong only to God. The cruel, Augustine says, desire to be feared but only God should be feared. In the same way, sloth desires rest but there is no rest outside of God, and luxury desires "plenty and abundance" but God is the "fullness and the unfailing plenty of incorruptible pleasure."[19]

In Augustine's words, we see one of the basic reasons why we flee from humility and therefore flee from repentance—we have a tendency to want to fulfill our desires in the way we choose. To say it another way, if even more directly, we desire to have what we want, when we want it, and in the way we want it. It is not simply our desire for material things but our desire to have the glory that should go to God. Instead of humility, our desires lead us to self-exaltation and pride. Chasing these desires leads us to turn away from God, and because we don't want to give up what we desire, our pride stands as a block to the humility that draws us to return to God.

Repentance, seen as an action of spiritual formation, where we turn down ourselves in humility and turn away from self-exaltation and pride, places us in the right position before God. In that proper place, we see ourselves for who we truly are, and rediscover that we only find genuine pleasure in God. Putting ourselves in the proper position before God in humility is an action within the process of repentance and reminds us that spiritual formation and discipleship begin with humility. Louis E. Newman, writing on repentance from a Jewish perspective, summarizes our discussion well: "To engage in *teshuvah* [repentance], psychologically speaking, is to come home to our truest selves. It is to cultivate profound self-awareness and do the inner work necessary to overcome all the fragmentation that prevents us from living fully."[20]

17. Augustine, *Confessions*, 58.

18. Watson calls this the "bewitching pleasure of sin." Watson, *Doctrine of Repentance*, 54.

19. Augustine, *Confessions*, 72.

20. Newman, *Repentance*, 113.

Turning to Forgiveness

What then does a humble and repentant church look like? What characteristic defines a church that sees itself as it really is and knows it's truest self? The answer is forgiveness. If we, as God's people, allow humility to lead us to repentance, the effect will be a well of forgiveness in action that will be irresistible to those in the world who still need to turn to God. Additionally, as we saw in chapter 5, the need for repentance includes Christians as well. Therefore, the church will also be forgiving toward fellow Christians who turn away from God and invite them to return and realign with God. When we are humble enough to understand we are fallen people and our nature is to turn away from God and when we turn away, each one of us needs to turn back to him, then we become forgiving of ourselves and forgiving of others.

In our current culture, forgiveness operates on either side of vast extremes. At times forgiveness is given based on the perceived worth of the individual who committed the offense. If the individual can score touchdowns on the football field or is a star on the basketball court, or if we enjoy watching the individual bring our favorite characters to life on the big screen, our culture is more likely to forgive even serious wrongdoing. The same goes for individuals who lead in business or politics, or those who have affluence or power. On the other extreme is the "cancel culture" that makes any wrong as a reason to permanently remove someone, regardless of their position or influence. As C. S. Lewis says, "Every one [*sic*] says forgiveness is a lovely idea, until they have something to forgive . . . and then, to mention the subject at all is to be greeted with howls of anger."[21] What is so confusing is our culture shows little to no consistency in who gets a pass and who gets cancelled.

Driscoll and Mars Hill, as well as Bill Hybels and Willow Creek Church, offer examples. Mike Cosper in *The Rise and Fall of Mars Hill* and Scot McKnight and Laura Barringer in *A Church Called Tov*[22] show a pattern within Mars Hill and Willow Creek, respectively, of giving passes, at the very least, on Driscoll's and Hybels's questionable behavior because they were gifted preachers, good leaders, and could point to plenty of "success" in ministry. Therefore, behavior that should have been addressed so pride could be put away and humility and repentance could be sought and found was allowed to fester until it resulted in the fall of Driscoll and Hybels and, more importantly, damage to at least two churches.

Miroslav Volf describes two possible ways we can deal with wrongdoing. The first way is to "neutralize wrongdoing" by somehow being able to

21. C. S. Lewis, *Mere Christianity*, 115.
22. See McKnight and Barringer, *Church Called Tov*, 1–4, 41–53.

undo the deed.[23] The second way is if the wrongdoing is somehow not our fault and therefore we carry no blame for the wrong deed.[24] However, both of these are impossible because "time doesn't run backward, and a done deed cannot be undone" and "harm suffered by the negligence or the intentional act of another is imputable to the one who had done it."[25] Thus, says Volf, "the wrongdoing sits like a burden on the shoulders of the one who has committed it."[26] Therefore, as our churches desire to move into God's mission in the world, and we come face to face with wrongdoing and sin in the lives of those we are reaching, we cannot merely give it a pass as though it never happened, nor can we cancel the person who has committed the wrongdoing; rather we help lead them to repentance.

Volf goes on to note, for Christians, forgiveness occurs within the triangular relationship of God, us, and the offender.[27] Forgiveness, then, like repentance occurs within the context of relationship. Rather than the transactional relationship that has come to describe much of American evangelicalism today,[28] where repentance can be seen as the trade we make for forgiveness, true repentance occurs within relationship, and so does true forgiveness. We see here how humility is essential to forgiveness, and both are tied to repentance. When we can put down our pride and our desire to get what we want (which when it comes to the offense of another is often revenge) and we turn ourselves down in humility (and in imitation of God, who is humble), then we are in the position to be forgiving and thus live out and help others toward repentance.

The church is called to stand in contrast to the way forgiveness is practiced, or rather many times not practiced, in our culture today. We don't forgive based upon what someone can do or the perceived worth they have. Nor do we refuse to forgive. Instead, because we know we ourselves are sinners and we have humbled ourselves before God and turned to him, we forgive because that is what God, in Jesus Christ, has done for us (Eph 4:32; Col 3:13).

23. Volf, *Free of Charge*, 128.

24. Volf, *Free of Charge*, 129.

25. Volf, *Free of Charge*, 129.

26. Volf, *Free of Charge*, 129.

27. Volf, *Free of Charge*, 131.

28. Wingfield defines transactional religions: "Transactional faith says if we do one thing God wants, God will in turn do what we want. Or the opposite: God makes an offer to us, and we must accept the terms of the contract in order to get the heavenly reward." Wingfield, "How Transactional Faith," paragraph 6.

TURNING AROUND: LOVE

Developing a character of humility, what we have called "turning down," so we can be forgiving precedes turning around. Once we have turned down and humbled ourselves, we are in the proper spiritual position to turn around in love to God, who himself is love, and turn in love toward others. As agents of repentance, we follow God's example and turn in love toward others, as God has turned toward us. The purpose of our turning in love to others is to lead them to turn in repentance to God. Ultimately love stands as the reason why we want to turn back or return to God. Love is also how we turn to God. Our turning comes as a response to God, who loved us and turned toward us in Jesus Christ. As we said, no one wants or likes to see themselves as a sinner, but when we realize the height and depth and length and width of God's love for us (Rom 8:38–39; Eph 3:18), while we were sinners (Rom 5:8), our response is to turn around in love to him. Thus, we turn around in love, to be united in love, to the one who is love.

Let's look at the link between repentance and love. Richard Owen Roberts rightfully states, "the everlasting love of God is a precious truth that undergirds the whole biblical doctrine of repentance."[29] In a similar vein Thomas Watson, writing on love and repentance, makes a powerful statement:

> Acts of sin may be restrained out of fear or design—but a true penitent turns from sin out of a pious principle, namely, out of love to God. Even if sin did not bear such bitter fruit—if death did not grow on this tree—a gracious soul would forsake sin, out of love to God. This is the most easy [sic] turning from sin. When things are frozen and congealed, the best way to separate them is by fire. When men and their sins are congealed together, the best way to separate them is by the fire of love. Three men, asking one another what made them leave sin: one said, "I think of the joys of heaven!" Said the second, "I think of the torments of hell!" But the third said, "I think of the love of God, and that makes me forsake sin!" How shall I offend the God of love?[30]

Love leads us away from God and toward sins, and love also leads us to turn around and return to God. When we turn to God, God receives us back in love. Nowhere do we see this more clearly than within the Parable of the Prodigal Son, which we find in Luke 15:11–32.

In his work on the Parable of the Prodigal Son, Henri Nouwen frames each step in the journey of the younger son in terms of love. As he describes

29. Roberts, *Repentance*, 164.
30. Watson, *Doctrine of Repentance*, 25–26.

the son's leaving, Nouwen admits he also has "fled the hands of blessing and run off to faraway places searching for love."[31] Later he continues this thought, saying, "The world's love is and always will be conditional. As long as I keep looking for my true self in the world of conditional love, I will remain 'hooked' to the world—trying, failing, and trying again . . . I am the prodigal son every time I search for unconditional love where it cannot be found."[32]

Nouwen says we need love. We were created to need it, as Thomas Merton says: "To say that I am made in the image of God is to say that love is the reason for my existence, for God is love."[33] However, when we seek the fulfillment of such a love outside of God, we act in sin. The beginning of sin is not found in hate or the desire to do evil; rather the beginning of sin is love, specifically the search for love, and even more specifically the search for unconditional love outside of God. Our search for love causes us to turn away from God, but love is also the means that leads us to turn around and turn toward God again.

We continue to see this in Nouwen's commentary on the prodigal son. As the younger son sits in the filthy and dehumanizing conditions of the pig pen, he comes to his senses and decides to return to his father. This is a repentance moment and it leads to a repentance process—as every step the son takes on his way home is a step of repentance. We discuss the process of repentance more fully in the final section of this chapter. As Nouwen examines the story, he concludes that love is central to his turning around:

> When he found himself desiring to be treated as one of the pigs, he realized that he was not a pig but a human being, a son of his father . . . Once he had come again in touch with the truth of his sonship, he could hear-although faintly—the voice calling him the Beloved and feel—although distantly—the touch of blessing. This awareness of and confidence in his father's love, misty as it may have been, gave him the strength to claim for himself his sonship, even though that claim could not be based on any merit.[34]

In Nouwen's view, the son turns around because he still has faith in his father's love for him—an unconditional love, not based on any merit the son has earned. Additionally, the son turns around because of his love for

---

31. Nouwen, *Prodigal Son*, 39.

32. Nouwen, *Prodigal Son*, 43.

33. Merton, *New Seeds of Contemplation*, 60.

34. Nouwen, *Prodigal Son*, 49. It could be said that the son no longer saw himself as a son of his father. I understand, however, Nouwen's interpretation to be correct. The son said he was not worthy of his sonship, and wished to be made like the hired servants. He did not deny that he was still his father's son.

his father. If Nouwen's observations and arguments are true, we can easily connect these dots. Nouwen goes on to suggest we can see Jesus within the younger son: "The prodigal becomes the return of the Son of God who has drawn all people into himself and brings them home to his heavenly Father."[35]

Throughout John's gospel, Jesus repeatedly references the Father's love for him. In John 14:31, however, Jesus speaks of his love for the Father. Jesus is speaking of his coming death and his return to the Father. He says, "I will not speak much more with you, for the ruler of the world is coming, and he has nothing in Me; but so that the world may know that I love the Father, I do exactly as the Father commanded Me" (14:30–31). If Jesus can be seen in the younger son, then the reason for his turn around must be love. And what else would it be? The younger son loves the father and realizes he cannot continue to live in a way that dishonors him. It is a turning around in love, just as Thomas Watson describes in the quote above.

The object of our love can lead us to turn away from God, but it also leads us to turn around toward God, as God becomes the object of our love. In our turning to God, we also discover love defines the character of the God to whom we turn. "The Father," Nouwen writes, "wants simply to let them [his children] know that the love they searched for in such distorted ways has been, is, and always will be there for them."[36] The love of God remains because, as John tells us, "God is love" (1 John 4:8). God's love leads us to the God who is love. We know God is love but we cannot love the statement "God is love" alone. We must first and foremost love the God who is love.[37] It is our love for God, who loved us first, that draws us to turn around and walk home to him in repentance when we search for love outside of God.

When we find ourselves fully encompassed within the love of God, we experience what the Christian mystics call "union with Christ." Union with Christ originates in love, "for it is love alone that unites and joins the soul with God."[38] Evangelicals may be hesitant of this concept, but when we realize we are already united with Christ and are already in him, what the mystics describe as "union with Christ" stands as a deeper realization of a truth that already exists.

While faith and hope also help the believer to turn around toward God, John of the Cross proposes that love "causes greater love in the Beloved [and] not only protects the soul and hides it from the third enemy, which is the flesh (for where there is true love of God there enter neither

35. Nouwen, *Prodigal Son*, 56.

36. Nouwen, *Prodigal Son*, 96.

37. See Coe and Strobel, *Embracing Contemplation*, 142.

38. John of the Cross, *Dark Night*, 92.

love of self nor that of the things of self), but even gives worth to the other virtues."[39] As we've already seen, the turning from self-love and the things of the self is repentance—the turning down of ourselves in humility before God. John of the Cross builds upon this and tells us turning around in love to God is another place marker in the process of repentance.

Turning in Love

Understanding how love draws us to repentance allows us, as individuals and church communities, to be loving. This should not come as a radical conclusion. However, sometimes we need to be reminded of the most basic foundational truths. After all, our love for one another declares to the world that we are disciples of Jesus (John 13:35). As disciples of Jesus, we are sent to preach the message of the gospel—including repentance in Jesus' name. The question is: does love define our gospel message? And does our message of repentance sound like the gospel? Is love the reason we want others to turn to God and unite their lives with him?

A message of love does not preach the gospel by means of coercion, manipulation, guilt, or shame, but rather from a genuine love for those who still need Jesus.[40] This love is not an emotion, as C. S. Lewis states: "It is a state not of feelings but of the will; that state of the will which we have naturally about ourselves, and must learn to have about other people."[41] If we wait for others to be loveable and thus for us to have the emotion of love, that will probably never happen. Rather, we must decide that because God is love, and we have experienced God's love in the person of Jesus Christ, and we have in love turned toward God in him, then our response to God's love is to love others regardless of their ability to be lovable. The same love that drew us to turn to God when we had turned away, and still calls us to return to God when we turn to love other things, is still calling those around us who still need to turn and be united with God. As the church, we are to be proclaimers of that love and witnesses to that union with Christ.

Living within love and in union with Christ comes as we turn around and turn toward him and turn away from all the idols vying for our love and attention. As the people of God, we understand how easily we turn away and chase after the things we substitute for God. As we grow in our identity as children of God, we must realize our past sin does not define our identity in Jesus. Understanding our identity as children of God in Jesus and as citizens

39. John of the Cross, *Dark Night*, 101.

40. See Keller, *Preaching*, 158–60.

41. C. S. Lewis, *Mere Christianity*, 129.

of the kingdom of God allows us to be diligent in removing sin from our lives while allowing us to be loving and compassionate toward ourselves and, just as importantly, loving toward others.

To see what this love looks like in practice, we need look no further than Jesus. As we examine the ministry of Jesus, we find his love is shown in his compassion. In Mark 6:34, Jesus sees the crowds and feels compassion for them because they "were like sheep without a shepherd." Jesus' compassion moves him to an action of love as he feeds the crowd, providing for their physical needs. John's gospel makes clear that Jesus' feeding of the crowd is itself a living parable looking ahead to the cross, where Jesus' compassion for those who are spiritually lost and needy culminates in the ultimate act of love—the giving of his body like broken bread (John 6:26–58).

A similar scene is found in Matthew 14:14, where Jesus again sees a crowd and, being moved to compassion, heals the sick among them. This is truly an act of love toward needy and broken people. As Jesus embodies the kingdom of God, he shows that love and acts of compassion go hand in hand. To follow Jesus' example means turning to those who, like the crowds that surrounded Jesus, appear broken and perhaps even unlovable, and telling them the gospel message—that God loves them and that though through Jesus they can turn to God be forgiven of their sin.

TURNING TOWARD: THE DISCIPLESHIP JOURNEY

We began by making the observation that the goal of discipleship and spiritual formation is to be (re)formed into the image of Christ. This forming, as we have seen, involves repentance—the repentance of turning down in humility and turning around in love. Continuing with the turning image, we also see repentance as a continual turning toward—a turning toward God as we become more fully (re)formed into the image of Christ. Here is where we truly focus on the process of repentance and how it moves us in discipleship to become more like Jesus. In the end, the purpose of repentance is to realign us with God and his purposes and mission, allowing us to become more like Jesus, as we engage in the process.

As much as we can define repentance as the point of coming to our senses and choosing to return to our Father, we must also see repentance as the whole journey from "pig pen to banquet table."[42] This process, or journey,

---

42. Utilizing Jesus' Story of the Lost Son in Luke 15, "pig pen to banquet table" summarizes the journey of the lost son from the moment he turns toward his father, through the journey (process) of returning home, and culminating in the celebration of his return at the banquet table.

of repentance forms us into the image of Christ. As we make this journey, we make at least three journeys simultaneously. We make the journey of repentance as a sinner, as a pilgrim, and as a leader. Let's look at each in turn.

As believers we know we are, paradoxically, free from sin, dead to sin, and alive in Christ. At the same time, we remain within a world where sin remains and in a body still capable of committing sins. Even our church communities struggle with the temptation to turn from God, and they put any number of things before him. Thus, as long as we are in this world, we will continually need to return to God and realign with him in repentance, as both saints and sinners.

Within the Parable of the Prodigal Son, we clearly see the younger son walk the road of repentance as a sinner. He confesses, "Father, I have sinned against heaven and in your sight; I am no longer worthy to be called your son" (Luke 15:21). The younger son's sin is the starting point on the journey of repentance. His turning away actually sets the stage for his turning down, turning around, and turning toward. As Richard Rohr notes, "Sin and salvation are correlative terms. Salvation is not sin perfectly avoided, as the ego would prefer; but in fact, salvation is sin turned on its head and used in our favor."[43] The graces of repentance and salvation take the sin that should eternally separate us from God and uses it as a way to teach us about God's character as well as form us into the image of Christ, as we take off the characteristics of the flesh and put on the characteristics of righteousness (Gal 5:16–23; Col 3:5–17).

Rohr goes on to say our goal as sinners on this journey of repentance should not be "sin management" but "sin transformation."[44] It may seem incorrect to think of sin transforming us; however, Rohr does give us much-needed wisdom, even while we must keep the apostle Paul's words in Romans 6:1–2 and 6:12–14 in mind as well.[45] Rohr does not advocate continuing to pursue sin; however, when we do sin, we need to see it as "something to be pitied and healed much more than hated, denied, or perfectly avoided."[46] When seen in this light, our sins can be tools of teaching—as we

43. Rohr, *Falling Upward*, 58.

44. Rohr, *Falling Upward*, 59.

45. Romans 6:1–2, "What shall we say then? Are we to continue in sin so that grace may increase? May it never be! How shall we who died to sin still live it?

Romans 6:12–14, "Therefore do not let sin reign in your mortal body so that you obey its lusts, and do not go on presenting the members of your body to sin as instruments of unrighteousness; but present yourselves to God as those alive from the dead, and your members as instruments of righteousness to God. For sin shall not be master over you, for you are not under law but under grace."

46. Rohr, *Falling Upward*, 59.

learn from them and God uses them to teach us. Rohr advises, "God seems to be about 'turning' our loves around and using them toward the Great love that is their true object."[47]

The process of walking home in repentance teaches us how, in the anonymous words of the author of *The Way of a Pilgrim*, "to love [God], as [we] have loved sin in the past."[48] As we learn how to love God more than the sin we have previously loved, despite our continual failures, we discover forgiveness. Rohr speaks to this directly, saying, "Falling, losing, failing, transgression, and sin are the pattern, I am sorry to report. Yet they all lead toward home."[49] But even before we get home, we find forgiveness. In the parable, the father does not decide to forgive when the son reaches home; he decides to forgive as soon as the son leaves. As we've said, the walk home is a walk of repentance but it is also a walk of forgiveness. He walks home a forgiven man, even though he does not know it yet.

Prayer is foundational to this journey. The main subject of *The Way of a Pilgrim* is prayer and prayer's power to change the life of the pilgrim and those he meets as he travels. Within the opening pages, the pilgrim asks a wise old man how he can pray without ceasing. The man answers in part, "Without prayer [the Christian] can not [sic] find the way to the Lord, he cannot understand the truth, he cannot crucify the flesh with its passions and lusts, his heart cannot be enlightened with the light of Christ, he cannot be savingly united to God."[50] This anonymous old man speaking to the anonymous pilgrim makes a correct theological statement: prayer is the foundation of spiritual formation.

Prayer is also the foundation to repentance. In the Old Testament and New Testament, we see turning linked to prayer. We see this within Solomon's prayer of dedication at the temple in 1 Kings 8 and 2 Chronicles 6. When Acts describes the early church as devoting itself to "the apostles' teaching and to fellowship, to the breaking of bread and to prayer" (Acts 2:42), I wonder if some of those prayers were prayers of repentance. As they read their Scripture, our Old Testament, it certainly seems probable to me they followed the example of Solomon, Nehemiah, and the Psalms and filled their prayers with repentance.

We cannot make the journey of repentance and live in humility, forgiveness, and love without prayer. Prayer moves us out of the place of control and allows God to be the one rightfully in that place. In prayer, our

47. Rohr, *Falling Upward*, 59.

48. *Way of a Pilgrim*, 47.

49. Rohr, *Falling Upward*, 64.

50. *Way of a Pilgrim*, 9.

desires, needs, and requests become aligned with God. Prayer is one of the most basic ways in which we respond to God and develop relationship with God. Both of these, as we saw in chapter 4, are pieces of what it means to repent. The Anglican Church, for example, has recently published a liturgy that includes corporate prayers and responsive readings centered on confession and repentance.[51] In several places the prayers in the Anglican liturgy address themes similar to what we have discussed so far. For example, one corporate prayer reads:

> O Christ,
> your body is stretched and torn
> by your friends who cannot befriend each other.
> We bring long-held grudges
> and recent grievances,
> and we chew them over,
> even at the foot of your cross.
> We tiptoe around chasms of misunderstanding,
> we pick our way anxiously
> among stumbling-blocks
> of language and culture,
> and blame each other
> for every mis-step,
> even while singing of your Spirit.
> We tremble to name the troubles we see
> in the Church and the world,
> for fear of our own sins finding us out,
> for fear that we will become easy targets
> for everyone's hostility.
> Have pity on us,
> for our hands are not strong enough
> and our hearts are not big enough
> to hold all together in love.
> When will you come to us,
> foolish as we are,
> downcast and despairing?
> When will you send us a breath of your Spirit
> with the perfume of resurrection and hope?[52]

Prayers like this, or similar prayers from other Christian traditions, are easy to adapt for our evangelical churches. They provide a way for us to think and talk about repentence and then pray prayers of repentance together.

51. See Anglican Consultative Council, *Season of Repentance.*
52. Anglican Consultative Council, *Season of Repentance,* 11.

Another example of how we can illustrate the journey of repentance comes from David Bentley Hart. Baptism ceremonies within the early church often included a physical turning. Hart reports how the baptizand would enter the water and face in one direction (often toward the west) and renounce his or her old way of life. After this renunciation, "Then he or she would turn to face the east (the land of the morning and of light) to confess total faith in, and promise complete allegiance to, Christ."[53] This act of turning "was by no means mere ritual spectacle; it was an actual and, so to speak, legally binding transference of fealty from one master to another."[54] This kind of physical turning is a powerful act our churches can also adapt and use, not only in our baptisms but also during worship or times of confession and corporate prayer.

As we move along the journey of repentance on our way back home, we make the journey not just as sinners, but as pilgrims. Being a pilgrim means more than simply singing, "This world is not my home, I'm just a passing thru."[55] If we take the pilgrim in *The Way of a Pilgrim* as an example, we begin to understand that being a pilgrim doesn't involve leaving the world but rather learning to truly live in it in the way that God desires. This is integral as we seek to live in the *missio Dei*—as the people of God in the mission of God. *The Way of a Pilgrim* tells the story of an unnamed pilgrim in Russia who surrenders to travel the countryside for the purpose of experiencing God. This pilgrim lives free of materialism and worry as he has dedicated himself to seek God wherever God might lead him. He is not tied to anything, and thus he can be bound tightly with his Lord.

What a beautiful picture of what the church can be in this world today! The effects that the temptations of power, money, and influence can have upon the church stand in stark contrast to the way of the pilgrim. The pilgrim church can live unbound to the materialism and worry of the world and be able to move freely wherever God would have her to go and to stay with whomever God would have her stay. The pilgrim church is the church walking the road of repentance on the journey home to God. We see in the life of the unnamed pilgrim two important traits of living as a pilgrim and as a church able and eager to engage the world in the mission of repentance: a pilgrim continuously moves and a pilgrim continuously prays.

We mentioned both movement and prayer in the previous section as we saw the movement along the journey of repentance. In the life of the pilgrim, we see another aspect of movement—the movement of following

---

53. Hart, *Atheist Delusions*, 113.

54. Hart, *Atheist Delusions*, 113.

55. Brumley, "This World Is Not My Home."

God's direction. Throughout the pilgrim's story, he remains in constant motion, moving from one town to another, all the while seeking God's leading and direction. As God leads, he continuously finds his physical needs met and his spiritual hunger satisfied. He also discovers his love for God and his knowledge of God grows. Whatever he does, whether walking or eating or drinking, he does with God at the center (1 Cor 10:31). He uses his whole life as a turning toward God—which, as we've noted, defines repentance. Additionally, prayer, for us as pilgrims and as part of a pilgrim church, is one of the foundational pieces to living the repentance mission. As pilgrims, we turn toward God in movement and prayer as we proceed on the journey of repentance.

Lastly, we turn toward God to be formed into the image of Jesus as leaders. Many people may not consider themselves leaders. I define a leader as anyone who has someone watching what he or she does. This expands leaders beyond CEOs, managers, and team captains. Parents are leaders. So are older siblings, classmates, Sunday school teachers, and the one giving a presentation in a board meeting. It also makes the entire church a leader, as the world around us watches how we live, love, and minister. As we make the journey of repentance from "pig pen to banquet table," if anyone is watching our journey, we make the journey as a leader, and as a leader we mark the way for others to follow. How then do we make the repentance journey as leaders?

Dan Allender suggests we make the journey with a "limp." The limp is the ability to acknowledge our mistakes.[56] Allender writes, "to the degree you face and name and deal with your failures as a leader, to that same extent you will create an environment conducive to growing and retaining productive and committed colleagues."[57] I would rephrase the previous statement to say, to the degree you face and name and deal with your failures as a leader, to that same extent you will give others a roadmap to follow to make their own turning back toward God. Allender makes a similar point: "Every believer is called to help someone grow into maturity—and such is the core calling of a leader."[58]

How does this happen? Essentially, Allender proposes we live our lives as a testimony to both our failures and God's grace. He says, "Here is God's leadership model: he chooses fools to live foolishly in order to reveal the economy of heaven, which reverses and inverts the wisdom of this world."[59]

56. Allender, *Leading with a Limp*, 3.

57. Allender, *Leading with a Limp*, 2.

58. Allender, *Leading with a Limp*, 25.

59. Allender, *Leading with a Limp*, 55.

Allender says we show off our limp. Our limp is the result of an encounter with God, an encounter where we "will not come out [of it] the same" and we "will walk a new path—with an unpredictable gait."[60] The act of repentance involves an encounter with God. We must see where we have turned from him and become out of line with him; then, like the lost son, we turn back to God and encounter him in a fresh way. Our journey and our experience with God may leave us with a limp we can use to help others. We can acknowledge how we turned from God and also tell the story of how we turned back.

We see this pattern within Augustine's *Confessions*. In that work, Augustine opens himself up before God and the reader. We are able to hear about his mistakes, his lusts, and his struggles toward faith. By following Augustine on his journey toward God, and using his journey as an example, we are led to discover God for ourselves and turn toward him. We find similar examples in the life of the anonymous pilgrim or the anonymous writer of *The Cloud of Unknowing*. Both of these leaders invite us to follow them on the journey toward God. As we do, we then become leaders and churches for others to follow. As Paul tells the Corinthian church, "Be imitators of me, just as I also am of Christ" (1 Cor 11:1).

What if we saw our story of turning away and turning back, what we can call our "limp," as one of the fruits of repentance? This fruit of repentance could be what helps others to turn back to God. The same is true for our churches. Our churches have an opportunity to tell their stories of repentance, rather than trying to sweep wrongs under the rug.

One way this can look for our churches is similar to what a group of college students did on the campus of the University of North Carolina–Wilmington. Influenced by Donald Miller's book *Blue Like Jazz*, students involved in the Christian group InterVarsity created a confessional booth; however, "rather than hearing confessions, the Christians confessed, apologizing for apathy, hostility or ignorance in the name of Christ, or the lack of concern for the environment, sex trafficking and other issues."[61] What if we, in a similar fashion, confessed our limps? Whether it is a history of racism, attitudes of pride or unforgiveness, or a failure of loving the people around us, our churches can become agents of repentance by acknowledging those mistakes and modeling the way of turning back to God.

Much has been made recently about the way Christians and the church tend to hide our true selves and live within the projection of reality we have made for ourselves. This is one of the themes explored in *The Rise and Fall*

---

60. Allender, *Leading with a Limp*, 48.

61. Sidell, "Confession in Reverse," paragraph 3.

of Mars Hill. Neither Mark Driscoll nor Mars Hill Church could admit where they were wrong or had made a mistake. As documented by Cosper, in almost every instance, Mars Hill and Driscoll maintained they were in the right and were doing what God wanted them to do, and everyone else must move to align with them. How different could their story have been if, instead of modeling pride and arrogance, they led by limping and in how to repent and turn back to God?

CONCLUSION

Throughout this chapter we have discovered the characteristics we need to be agents of repentance, both as individuals and as church communities. We have also gained an image of what the church can become if it embodies repentance. A church that embodies repentance as it accompanies God in his mission will be forgiving, loving, and disciple-making. When we turn to God, we are then able to forgive others, understanding they also need to turn to God. We will also be loving and turn to others in love as we call them to turn to God through the gospel. Finally, we will be disciple-making as we understand repentance is a process, a journey, we make as sinners, pilgrims, and leaders, throughout our whole lives.

Our whole lives are a walk home. We do not repent once and then never need to repent again. Rather, because we continually stray like sheep, we continually need to return, but we return within the journey home—toward God's ultimate ends and toward the vision of perfect relationship with God and with one another we see in Revelation 21. Our whole life becomes a life of repentance and of returning and realigning with God. We don't need to be ashamed or hide that we are constantly on the journey of repentance. Rather, because we see repentance as part of God's mission, part of our mission as the church, and something we will continue to live out our whole life on earth, we can live in the process and journey of repentance. This process involves turning down in humility and living in forgiveness, turning around to God in love and turning in love to a lost world, and turning toward the journey of repentance as a part of becoming more like Jesus.

Conclusion

TURNING OUT

As we conclude this work, let's review the road we've traveled. This entire study has been built upon the recognition that something is wrong in the way the American evangelical church has approached its mission. We have mission statements. We know we are to go and make disciples, but instead we've seen our churches in a state of decline persisting for over two decades. The proposal of this work is one reason the church is not growing as men and women come to know Christ is because we have forgotten a vital piece of the church's mission—repentance. Instead of turning and realigning ourselves with God, the version of Christianity too often seen and too many times preached is an individualized Christianity where we can pick and choose the parts we like and discard the parts we don't. Thus, the version of Christianity all too often experienced in American evangelical churches today is a Christianity that has succumbed to the times rather than transforming the times.

My hope in this work is threefold. First, I hope to leave the reader with a clearer understanding of the doctrine of repentance. We have achieved this by building upon the labor of those who have written on the topic of repentance previously. While I have noted places of disagreement, much of our understanding of repentance remains aligned overall. I have also sought to continue the discussion of my predecessors by advancing it into an area that has not, as of yet, been explored in detail—which is the connection between repentance and mission. I have explored this uncharted dimension of repentance and have shown how repentance and preaching the message of repentance is central to the mission of the church because it is central to God's mission, the *missio Dei*, the mission of Jesus, and in turn the mission of Peter, Paul, and the early church.

My second hope is to show the reader the connection between repentance and discipleship. Throughout the final three chapters of this work, examples were given to help us put the mission of repentance into practice within the life of the church. These are merely the beginning of the ways we can become agents of repentance within the world.

Third, I hope to demonstrate how preaching and practicing repentance is vital for the church to be able to carry out its mission in the world. No matter what good is done by our church ministries and activities, if we are not calling all people to turn/return, and realign with God, we are missing a part of what we are called to do as the church of Jesus Christ. This is truly the heart of the matter.

In part 1, after we surveyed the current landscape of scholarly writing on repentance, we established God's mission in the world is for a people to turn to him. We saw this is central to the *missio Dei* and is seen throughout the Old Testament. God's call for his people to turn/return to him begins in Genesis in God's covenant to Abraham, is included in the promise of the promised land, and appears throughout the messages of the prophets. Moving to the New Testament, we continued to note this mission in the life and ministry of Jesus. We saw as Jesus comments on why he came, each mission statement is tied back to God's mission because Jesus came to complete God's mission in the world. Ultimately, Jesus came to make a way for us to turn/return to God.

In part 2, we began in chapter 4 by looking at the breadth of the meaning of repentance as we traced its use through the Old and New Testaments. We examined the Hebrew and Greek words used to connote repentance to understand the different ways turning to God is described throughout the biblical witness. From our survey we drew six defining pieces of repentance:

1. Repentance is a response to God.

2. Repentance brings evidence.

3. Repentance is for everyone.

4. Repentance is for sins.

5. Repentance saves from divine consequences.

6. Repentance occurs in the context of relationships.

In chapter 5, we turned our attention to the mission of the church. We saw proof our churches and our culture are in desperate need of hearing a message of repentance. As we looked at the example of the early church in Acts, we clearly saw repentance as a central piece of the church's mission. From this observation came the main emphasis of this work: repentance makes and moves the people of God into the mission of God. As we have said throughout, and emphasized again above, if repentance is part of God's mission, Jesus' mission, and the mission of the early church, surely it ought to be part of our mission today within the modern church.

In part 3, we moved to application and sought to discover how repentance and being agents of repentance as we continue the mission of God is part of the ultimate end God is moving all of creation toward. We saw how repentance is vital to the kingdom of God, including the transformation and the new reality inaugurated in the kingdom. Lastly, we examined the characteristics our churches will have as they embrace the repentance mission. We saw how repentance makes us and our churches humble and forgiving. Additionally, repentance is an act of love that makes us loving. Finally, repentance as a part of spiritual formation makes us disciple-making.

Before we conclude this work, I want to issue one more invitation. In the final chapter, we described repentance as turning down, turning around, and turning toward. Repentance also involves turning out. We mentioned this in several forms throughout this work, but it is the final message I want you, the reader, to hear. If we take the words in these pages to heart and truly turn to God and realign with him in our personal lives and in our churches, our own turning is only half of repentance. The other half requires us to go out from our churches to those still needing to turn to God. Our mission as the church is to call them to turn and come to God, to realign with him, to find forgiveness for their sins in Jesus' name, and to become a part of God's people. It is a message of repentance defined by a realigment with God in every part of their lives, not just the parts they pick and choose.

The reality, and even the irony, is when the church preaches the message of repentance within the wider gospel message, we proclaim something completely different than the world. It isn't a message that sin doesn't matter or that our sin causes a permanent "canceling"; rather, our message is when we turn to God, sin is forgiven. When we turn to God, we return and become the people we were created to be. When we turn to God, we are able to forgive the wrongs of others, we are able to love the unlovable, we are able to lead others to turn to God, and we are able to join God as he moves all of creation toward his ultimate ends. Instead of repentance being the scary, shameful, and guilt-inducing message I remember as a child, repentance is truly an amazing grace of God that allows us to come back to him when we have wandered and join him in his mission. As we turn down, turn around, and turn toward, let's not neglect to turn out and take the message of repentance into the world!

Bibliography

Alexander, Ralph H. *Ezekiel*. Expositor's Bible Commentary 6. Grand Rapids: Zondervan, 1986.

Allender, Dan B. *Leading with a Limp*. New York: WaterBrook, 2006.

AND Campaign. https://www.andcampaign.org/about.

Anglican Consultative Council. *A Season of Repentance*. 2020. https://www. anglicancommunion.org/media/355990/a-season-of-repentance-en.pdf.

Augustine. *The Confessions of Saint Augustine*. Translated by John K. Ryan. New York: Doubleday, 1960.

Bailey, Jon Nelson. "Repentance in Luke-Acts." PhD diss., University of Notre Dame, 1993.

Bailey, Sarah Pulliam, and Michelle Boorstein. "Several Black Pastors Break with the Southern Baptist Convention over a Statement on Race." *The Washington Post*, December 23,2020. https://www.washingtonpost.com/religion/2020/12/23/black -pastors-break-southern-baptist-critical-race-theory/.

Barna Group. "Self-Described Christians Dominate America but Wrestle with Four Aspects of Spiritual Depth." September 13, 2011. https://www.barna.com. research/self-described-christians-dominate-america-but-wrestle-with-four- aspects-of-spiritual-depth/.

Bautch, Richard J. "'May Your Eyes to Open and Your Ears Attentive': A Study of Penance and Penitence in the Writings." In *Repentance in Christian Theology*, edited by Mark J. Boda and Gordon T. Smith, 67–85. Collegeville, MN: Liturgical, 2006.

Black, Eric. "Even Bob Dylan Knows You Can't Serve Two Masters." *Baptist Standard*, December 21, 2021. https://www.baptiststandard.com/opinion/Editorials/even- bob-dylan-knows-you-cant-serve-two-masters/.

Boda, Mark J. "Renewal in Heart, Word, and Deed: Repentance in the Torah." In *Repentance in Christian Theology*, edited by Mark J. Boda and Gordon T. Smith, 3–24. Collegeville, MN: Liturgical, 2006.

———. *Return to Me: A Biblical Theology of Repentance*. New Studies in Biblical Theology. Downers Grove, IL: InterVarsity, 2015.

Boda, Mark J., and Gordon T. Smith, eds. *Repentance in Christian Theology*. Collegeville, MN: Liturgical, 2006.

Brooks, David. *The Second Mountain*. New York: Random House, 2019.

Brownlee, William H. *Ezekiel 1–19*. Word Biblical Commentary 28. Waco, TX: Word, 1986.

Brueggemann, Walter. "The Summons to New Life: A Reflection." In *Repentance in Christian Mission*, edited by Mark J. Boda and Gordon T. Smith, 347–69. Collegeville, MN: Liturgical, 2006.

Brumley, Albert E. "This World Is Not My Home (I'm Just a Passing Thru)." Public domain.

Calvin, John. *The Institutes of the Christian Religion*. Edited by Tony Lane and Hilary Osborne. Grand Rapids: Baker, 1986, 1987, 2006.

Chamberlain, William Douglas. *The Meaning of Repentance*. Philadelphia: Westminster, 1943.

Chatraw, Joshua. "Jesus' Theology of Repentance and Forgiveness as Both Individual and Corporate: A Response to N.T. Wright." PhD diss., Southeastern Baptist Theological Seminary, 2013.

Coe, John H., and Kyle C. Strobel, eds. *Embracing Contemplation: Reclaiming a Christian Spiritual Practice*. Downers Grove, IL: InterVarsity, 2019.

Cosper, Mike, editor and host. "Aftermath." *The Rise and Fall of Mars Hill*. Christianity Today, December 2021.

———. *The Rise and Fall of Mars Hill*. Podcast series. Christianity Today, 2021, 2022. https://www.christianitytoday.com/ct/podcasts/rise-and-fall-of-mars-hill/.

DeGroat, Chuck. *When Narcissism Comes to Church*. Downers Grove, IL: InterVarsity, 2020.

Dempsey, Carol J. "'Turn Back, O People': Repentance in the Latter Prophets." In *Repentance in Christian Theology*, edited by Mark J. Boda and Gordon T. Smith, 47–66. Collegeville, MN: Liturgical, 2006.

DiRocco, Michael. "Urban Meyer Apologizes Again, Says He Didn't Consider Resigning as Jacksonville Jaguars Coach." ESPN, October 6, 2021. https://www.espn.com/nfl/story/_/id/32348439/urban-meyer-says-never-considered-resigning-jacksonville-jaguars-coach.

Du Mez, Kristin Kobes. *Jesus and John Wayne: How White Evangelicals Corrupted a Faith and Fractured a Nation*. New York: Liveright, 2020.

Evans, Craig A. *Mark 8:27—16:20*. Word Biblical Commentary 34B. Nashville: Thomas Nelson, 2001.

Ferguson, Sinclair. *The Grace of Repentance*. Wheaton, IL: Crossway, 2010.

First Baptist Dallas. "Christmas Greeting from Donald J. Trump, 45th President of the United States, December 19, 2021." YouTube, December 20, 2021. https://youtube.com/watch?v=8QyDt8FhrMM.

Ford Motor Company. "Our Purpose." https://corporate.ford.com/about/purpose.html.

Fretheim, Terence E. "Repentance in the Former Prophets." In *Repentance in Christian Theology*, edited by Mark J. Boda and Gordon T. Smith, 25–45. Collegeville, MN: Liturgical, 2006.

Garber, Megan. "Sorry, Not Sorry: Why Public Figures Stopped Apologizing." *The Atlantic*, December 2019. https://www.theatlantic.com/magazine/Archive/2019/12/sorry-no-apologies/600742/.

Giboney, Justin. "Christian Virtue Strengthens the Social Justice Cause." *Christianity Today*, August 24, 2021. https://www.christianitytoday.com/ct/2021/august-web-only/racism-social-justice-christian-virtue-strengthens.html.

Gooder, Paula. *The Pentateuch: A Story of Beginnings*. London: T. & T. Clark, 2000.

Goodrick, Edward W., and John R. Kohlenberger III. *The NIV Exhaustive Concordance*. Grand Rapids: Zondervan, 1990.

Grogan, Geoffrey W. *Isaiah*. Expositor's Bible Commentary 6. Grand Rapids: Zondervan, 1986.

Guinness World Records. "Largest Buffet." https://www.guinnessworldrecords.com/world-records/largest.buffet.

Hägerland, Tobias. "Jesus and the Rites of Repentance." *New Testament Studies* 52 (2006) 166–87.

Harrison, Nonna Verna. *God's Many-Splendored Image*. Grand Rapids: Baker Academic, 2010.

Hart, David Bentley. *Atheist Delusions: The Christian Revolution and Its Fashionable Enemies*. New Haven, CT: Yale University Press, 2009.

Hawthorne, Gerald F., et al. *Dictionary of Paul and His Letters*. Downers Grove, IL: InterVarsity, 1993.

Hodges, Zane C. *Harmony with God: A Fresh Look at Repentance*. Dallas: Redencion Viva, 2001.

Humphrey, Edith M. "'And I Shall Heal Them': Repentance, Turning, and Penitence in the Johannine Writings." In *Repentance in Christian Theology*, edited by Mark J. Boda and Gordon T. Smith, 105–26. Collegeville, MN: Liturgical, 2006.

Janz, Denis R. *A Reformation Reader: Primary Texts with Introduction*. 2nd ed. Minneapolis: Fortress, 2008.

Jenkins, Jack. "Immigration Reform Used to Unite Faith Groups—Not Anymore." *Religion News Service*, February 4, 2022. https://religionnews.com/2022/02/04/immigration-reform-used-to-unite-faith-groups-not-anymore/.

John of the Cross. *Dark Night of the Soul*. Translated by E. Allison Peers. Mineola, NY: Dover, 2003.

Jones, Jeffery M. "U.S. Church Membership Down Sharply in Past Two Decades." Gallup, April 18, 2019. https://news.gallup.com/poll/248837/church-membership-down-sharply-past-two-decades.aspx.

Kärkkäinen, Veli-Matti. *An Introduction to Ecclesiology: Ecumenical, Historical & Global Perspectives*. Downers Grove, IL: IVP Academic, 2002.

Keller, Timothy. *Preaching: Communicating Faith in an Age of Skepticism*. New York: Viking, 2015.

Kierkegaard, Søren. *Attack upon "Christendom"*. Translated by Walter Lowrie. Princeton, NJ: Princeton University Press, 1968.

———. *Training in Christianity*. Translated by Walter Lowrie. Edited by John F. Thornton and Susan B. Varenne. New York: Vintage, 2004.

Kinnaman, David, and Gabe Lyons. *Unchristian: What a New Generation Really Thinks about Christianity . . . and Why It Matters*. Grand Rapids: Baker, 2007.

Kintu, Moses. "Repentance in the Sermon on the Mount." PhD diss., Trinity International University, 2014.

Koehler, Ludwig, and Walter Baumgartner. *The Hebrew and Aramaic Lexicon of the Old Testament*, vol. 2. Boston: Brill, 2001.

Komar, Marlen. "The Worst (and Best) Celebrity Apologies." *Livingly*, October 15, 2020. https://www.livingly.com/The+Worst+And+Best+Celebrity+Apologies.

Köstenberger, Andreas J., and T. Desmond Alexander. *Salvation to the Ends of the Earth: A Biblical Theology of Mission*. 2nd ed. New Studies in Biblical Theology. Downers Grove, IL: IVP Academic, 2020.

Ladd, George Eldon. *The Gospel of the Kingdom: Scriptural Studies in the Kingdom of God*. Paternoster, 1959. Reprint, Grand Rapids: Eerdmans, 2000.

Lee, ChoongJae. "Metánoia (Repentance): A Major Theme of the Gospel of Matthew." PhD diss., The Southern Baptist Theological Seminary, 2018.

Lee, Morgan. "Christian Nationalism Is Worse than You Think." *Quick to Listen*. Christianity Today, January 13, 2021. https://www.christianitytoday.com/ct/podcasts/quick-to-listen/Christian-nationalism-capitol-riots-trump-podcast.html.

Lewis, C. S. *Mere Christianity*. New York: HarperOne, 1980.

Lifeway Research. "The State of American Theology Study 2020." September 2020. http://research.lifeway.com/wp-content/uploads/2020/09/Ligonier-State-of-Theology-2020-Report.pdf.

Longenecker, Richard N. *Acts*. Expositor's Bible Commentary 9. Grand Rapids: Zondervan, 1981.

Lupfer, Jacob. "At First Baptist Dallas, White Evangelicals Line Up for Trump's Second Coming." *Religion News Service*, December 21, 2021. https://religionnews.com/2021/21/21/at-first-baptist-dallas-white-evangelicals-line-up-for-trumps-second-coming/.

Mann, Alan. *Atonement for a Sinless Society*. Eugene, OR: Cascade, 2015.

McKnight, Scot. *A Community Called Atonement*. Living Theology. Nashville: Abingdon, 2007.

McKnight, Scot, and Laura Barringer. *A Church Called Tov: Forming a Goodness Culture That Resists of Power and Promotes Healing*. Carol Stream, IL: Tyndale, 2020.

Meador, Jake. *In Search of the Common Good: Christian Fidelity in a Fractured World*. Downers Grove, IL: InterVarsity, 2019.

Merton, Thomas. *New Seeds of Contemplation*. New York: New Directions, 1961.

Miller, C. John. *Repentance: A Daring Call to Real Surrender*. Fort Washington, PA: CLC, 1975, 2019.

Miller, Paul D. "What Is Christian Nationalism?" *Christianity Today*, February 3, 2021. https://www.christianitytoday.com/ct/2021/february-web-only/what-is-christian nationalism.html.

Minear, Paul S. *Images of the Church in the New Testament*. Louisville: Westminster John Knox, 1960, 2004.

Moltmann, Jürgen. *The Church in the Power of the Spirit*. Minneapolis: Fortress, 1993.

———. *Theology of Hope: On the Ground and the Implications of a Christian Eschatology*. Minneapolis: Fortress, 1993.

———. *The Way of Jesus Christ*. Minneapolis: Fortress, 1993.

Morton, Heather. "Medical Professional Apologies Statues." National Conference of State Legislators, August 2, 2021. https://www.ncsl.org/research/financial-services-and commerce/medical-professional-apologies-statutes.aspx.

Myers, Allen C., ed. *The Eerdmans Bible Dictionary*. Grand Rapids: Eerdmans, 1987.

Nanakdewa, Kevin, et al. "The Salience of Choice Fuels Independence: Implications for Self-Perception, Cognition, and Behavior." *Proceedings of the National Academy of Sciences* 118:30 (July 27, 2021). https://www.pnas.org/content/118/30/e2021727118.

Nave, Guy Dale, Jr. "Repent, for the Kingdom of God Is at Hand:' Repentance in the Synoptic Gospels and Acts." In *Repentance in Christian Theology*, edited by Mark J. Boda and Gordon T. Smith, 87–103. Collegeville, MN: Liturgical, 2006.

———. *The Role and Function of Repentance in Luke–Acts*. Atlanta: Society of Biblical Literature, 2002.

Newbigin, Lesslie. *The Gospel in a Pluralist Society*. Grand Rapids: Eerdmans, 1989.

Newman, Louis E. *Repentance: The Meaning and Practice of Teshuvah*. Woodstock, VT: Jewish Lights, 2010.

Nike. "Impact: Taking Action." https://about.nike.com/en/impact.

Noll, Mark A. "Defining Evangelicalism." In *Global Evangelicalism: Theology, History and Culture in Regional Perspective*, edited by Donald M. Lewis and Richard V. Pierard, 17–37. Downers Grove, IL: IVP Academic, 2014.

Nouwen, Henri J.M. *The Return of the Prodigal Son*. New York: Doubleday, 1994.

Ortlund, Dane. *Gentle and Lowly: The Heart of Christ for Sinners and Sufferers*. Wheaton, IL: Crossway, 2020.

Ott, Craig. *The Church on Mission: A Biblical Vision for Transformation among All People*. Grand Rapids: Baker Academic, 2019.

Ovey, Michael J. *The Feasts of Repentance: From Luke–Acts to Systematic and Pastoral Theology*. New Studies in Biblical Theology. Downers Grove, IL: IVP Academic, 2019.

Perry, Samuel L. "The Deadly Dogmatism of Christian Nationalism." *Religion News Service*, January 28, 2022. https://religionnews.com/2022/01/28/the-deadly-dogmatism-of-christian-nationalism./

Pew Research Center. "In U.S., Decline of Christianity Continues at Rapid Pace: An Update on America's Changing Religious Landscape." October 17, 2019. https://www.pewforum.org/2019/10/17/in-u-s-decline-of-christianity-continues-at-rapid-pace/.

Porter, Stanley E. "Penitence and Repentance in the Epistles." In *Repentance in Christian Theology*, edited by Mark J. Boda and Gordon T. Smith, 127–50. Collegeville, MN: Liturgical, 2006.

Prosser, Maggie. "5 Takeaways from Trump's Morning at First Baptist Church." *The Dallas Morning News*, December 19, 2021. https://www.dallasnews.com/news/2021/12/19/5-takeaways-from-trumps-morning-at-first-baptist-church/.

Putman, Jim, and Bobby Harrington. *Discipleshift: Five Stages That Help Your Church to Make Disciples Who Make Disciples*. Grand Rapids: Zondervan, 2013.

Roberts, Richard Owen. *Repentance: The First Word of the Gospel*. Wheaton: Crossway, 2002.

Rohr, Richard. *Falling Upward: A Spirituality for the Two Halves of Life*. Large print ed. San Francisco: Jossey-Bass, 2011.

Schökel, Luis Alonso. "Isaiah." In *The Literary Guide to the Bible*, edited by Robert Alter and Frank Kermode, 165–83. Cambridge: Belknap Press of Harvard University Press, 1987.

Schroeder, George. "Seminary Presidents Reaffirm BFM, Declare CRT Incompatible." *Baptist Press*, November 30, 2020. https://www.baptistpress.com/resourcelibrary/news/seminary-presidents-reaffirms-bfm-declare-crt-incompatible/.

Shellnutt, Kate. "Former Mars Hill Elders: Mark Driscoll Is Still 'Unrepentant,' Unfit to Pastor." *Christianity Today*, July 26, 2021. https://www.christianitytoday.com/news/2021/july/mars-hill-elders-letter-mark-driscoll-pastor-resign-trinity.html.

———. "Southern Baptists See Biggest Drop in 100 Years." *Christianity Today*, June 4, 2020. https://www.christianitytoday.com/news/2020/june/southern-baptist-sbc-member-drop-annual-church-profile-2019.html.

Sidell, Mark. "Confession in Reverse at UNC-Wilmington." InterVarsity StudentSoul. https://studentsoul.intervarsity.org/confessional.

Smietana, Bob. "At Milwaukee Church, Refugees Find Welcome from a Less Suspicious Time." *Religion News Service*, January 10, 2022. https://religionnews. com/2022/01/10/at-eastbrook-church-in-milwaukee-friendship-and-a-warm-welcome-are-way-of-life-refugees-immigration-evangelicals/.

———. "Southern Baptist Decline Continues, Denomination Has Lost More than 2 Million Members since 2006." *Religion News Service*, May 21, 2021. https://religionnews.com/2021/05/21/southern-baptist-decline-continues-denomination-has-lost-more-than-2-mission-members-since-2006/.

Smith, Gordon T. "The Penitential: An Evangelical Perspective." In *Repentance in Christian Theology*, edited by Mark J. Boda and Gordon T. Smith, 267–86. Collegeville, MN: Liturgical, 2006.

Smith, Gregory A. "More White Americans Adopted than Shed Evangelical Label during Trump Presidency, Especially His Supporters." Pew Research Center, September 15, 2021. https://www.pewresearch.org/fact-tank/2021/09/15/more-white-americans-adopted-than-shed-evangelical-label-during-trump-presidency-especially-his-supporters/.

Smither, Edward L. *Mission in the Early Church: Themes and Reflections*. Eugene, OR: Cascade, 2014.

Sproul, R. C. *What Is Repentance?* Sanford, FL: Reformation Trust, 2014.

"A Statement on Justice, Repentance, and the SBC." December 18, 2020. https://www. justicerepentancesbc.org/statement.

Stewart, Emily. "Mario Batali's Sexual Misconduct Apology Came with a Cinnamon Roll Recipe." *Vox*, December 16, 2017. https://www.vox.com/2017/12/16/16784544/mario-batali-cinnamon-roll-apology.

Stokel-Walker, Chris. "How Smartphones and Social Media Are Changing Christianity." BBC, February 22, 2017. https://www.bbc.com/future/Article/20170222-how-smartphones-and-social-media-are-changing-religion.

Stump, Elenore. *Atonement*. Oxford: University Press, 2018.

Sunquist, Scott W. *Understanding Christian Mission: Participation in Suffering and Glory*. Grand Rapids: Baker Academic, 2013.

Swanson, David W. *Rediscipling the White Church: From Cheap Diversity to True Solidarity*. Downers Grove, IL: InterVarsity, 2020.

Sweeney, Douglas A. *The American Evangelical Story: A History of the Movement*. Grand Rapids: Baker Academic, 2005.

Tsioulcas, Anastasia, and Mandalit del Barco "'Ellen' Producers Face Another Round of Allegations, Including Sexual Misconduct." NPR, July 31, 2020. https://www.npr.org/2020/07/31/897646026/ellen-producers-face-another-round-of-allegations-including-sexual-misconduct.

Vanhoozer, Kevin J. *Faith Speaking Understanding: Performing the Drama of Doctrine*. Louisville: Westminster John Knox, 2014.

Veith, Gene Edward, Jr. *Post-Christian: A Guide to Contemporary Thought and Culture*. Wheaton, IL: Crossway, 2020.

Volf, Miroslav. *Free of Charge: Giving and Forgiving in a Culture Stripped of Grace*. Grand Rapids: Zondervan, 2005.

Watson, Thomas. *The Doctrine of Repentance*. Public domain.

Wax, Trevin K. "Eschatological Discipleship: Leading Believers to Understand Their Historical and Cultural Context." PhD diss., Southeastern Baptist Theological Seminary, 2015.

———. "On 'The Rise and Fall of Mars Hill'—Surveying Our Souls." The Gospel Coalition, September 28, 2021. https://www.thegospelcoalition.org/blogs/trevin-wax/rise-mars-hill/.

The Way of a Pilgrim. Translated by E. French. San Francisco: Harper, 1991.

Wenham, Gordon J. *Exploring the Old Testament: A Guide to the Pentateuch*. Vol. 1. Downers Grove, IL: InterVarsity, 2003.

———. *Genesis 1–15*. Word Biblical Commentary 1. Waco, TX: Word, 1987.

Wessel, Walter W. *Mark*. Expositor's Bible Commentary 8. Grand Rapids: Zondervan, 1984.

White, Randy. "Waves of Blessing, Waves of Change." Center for Christian Ethics at Baylor University, 2008. https://www.baylor.edu/content/services/document.php/66502.pdf.

Wilkin, Robert. "Repentance as a Condition for Salvation in the New Testament." ThD diss., Dallas Theological Seminary, 1985.

———. *Turn and Live: The Power of Repentance*. Denton, TX: Grace Evangelical Society, 2019.

Wingfield, Mark. "How Transactional Faith Led Evangelicals to Embrace Transactional Politics." *Baptist News Global*, December 1, 2020. https://baptistnews.com/article/how-transactional-faith-led-evangelicals-to-embrace-Transactional-politics/#.YgaPwC-B1KM.

Witherington, Ben, III. *Jesus, Paul, and the End of the World: A Comparative Study in New Testament Eschatology*. Downers Grove, IL: InterVarsity, 1992.

Wright, Christopher J. H. *The Mission of God: Unlocking the Bible's Grand Narrative*. Downers Grove, IL: IVP Academic, 2006.

Wright, N. T. *The Day the Revolution Began: Reconsidering the Meaning of Jesus' Crucifixion*. New York: HarperOne, 2016.

———. *How God Became King: The Forgotten Story of the Gospels*. New York: HarperOne, 2012.

———. *Jesus and the Victory of God*. Minneapolis: Fortress, 1996.

———. *The New Testament and the People of God*. Minneapolis: Fortress, 1992.

———. *The Resurrection and the Son of God*. Minneapolis: Fortress, 2003.

———. *Simply Christian: Why Christianity Makes Sense*. New York: HarperOne, 2006.

———. *Simply Jesus: A New Vision of Who He Was, What He Did, and Why It Matters*. New York: HarperOne, 2011.

———. *Surprised by Hope: Rethinking Heaven, the Resurrection, and the Mission of the Church*. New York: HarperOne, 2008.

Yandoli, Krystie Lee. "Former Employees Say Ellen's 'Be Kind' Talk Show Mantra Masks a Toxic Work Culture." *BuzzFeed News*, July 16, 2020. https://www.buzzfeednews.com/article/krystieyandoli/ellen-employees-allege-toxic-workplace-culture.